Cracking
the Zero Mystery

Cracking
the Zero Mystery

■

How the U.S.
Learned to Beat Japan's
Vaunted WWII Fighter Plane

■

Jim Rearden

Stackpole Books

Copyright © 1990 by Jim Rearden

Published by
STACKPOLE BOOKS
Cameron and Kelker Streets
P.O. Box 1831
Harrisburg, PA 17105

Printed in the United States of America

10 9 8 7 6 5 4 3 2 1

First Edition

Cover photo courtesy of the U.S. Navy.
Cover design by Tracy Patterson.
Interior design by Ellen C. Dawson.

Library of Congress Cataloging-in-Publication Data

Rearden, Jim.
    Cracking the Zero mystery : how the U.S. learned to beat Japan's vaunted WWII fighter plane / Jim Rearden.—1st ed.
       p.   cm.
    Includes bibliographical references.
    ISBN 0-8117-2235-X
    1. World War, 1939–1945—Aerial operations, Japanese. 2. Zero (Fighter planes) 3. World War, 1939–1945—Military intelligence—United States. I. Title.
D792.J3R43   1990
940.54′4952—dc20   89-38354
                              CIP

084879

Contents

Foreword

I first met Jim Rearden on the Aleutian island of Adak. Adak lies about halfway between the end of the Alaskan peninsula and the island of Attu at the outer, or western, end of the Aleutian chain of islands that stretches far out across the North Pacific Ocean.

Jim was returning from a writing assignment for *National Geographic* magazine at Kiska, 260 statute miles west of Adak. Kiska, American territory, was held by the Japanese during World War II for 14 months, and the carnage of war is very much in evidence there. Subjected to ever-increasing intensity of aerial bombardment, there is a litter of rusting hulks of ships, some grounded on the beaches and others on the bottom of Kiska Harbor. Ashore, guns—anti-aircraft and even coastal defense guns—rust in their emplacements. Tunnels, underground facilities, and trenches are everywhere.

Attu Island, 200 miles west of Kiska, was also occupied by the Japanese. Attu was retaken by an amphibious operation against the fanatical resistance of its 2,600-man garrison, 12–28 May 1943. Only 29 Japanese survived. Kiska was evacuated by the Japanese on 28 July 1943, using a force of two light cruisers and 10 destroyers operating under cover of dense fog. About two weeks later the force of 35,000 U.S. and Canadian troops who landed on Kiska found no Japanese there.

Attu lies almost exactly 1,000 statute miles west of Scotch Cap lighthouse at the tip of the Alaska peninsula. The southernmost island of the Aleutian chain, Amchitka, is only 250 miles north of the latitude of Seattle. The Aleutian Islands are treeless, but constant moisture gives them a lush covering of deep grass, which is hard to traverse on foot. In the spring the islands are a riot of colorful wild flowers. Flat spots in the terrain are usually bogs. Waterfalls are numerous, and streams run thick with salmon during the spawning season. The climate . . . is interesting. Since the colder water of the Bering Sea mixes with the warmer water of the North Pacific Ocean along the Aleutian Island chain, there are persistent fogs in the summer.

In the winter the Aleutian low barometric pressure area spawns howling storms. There are good days, mostly in the spring and fall, when one can see for many miles. The scenery is magnificent. Flying along, one passes one volcano after another, many of them smoking. Interestingly, in flying from Adak to Kiska one crosses the 180th meridian and goes from west longitude to east longitude. Agreement among the nations, however, has moved the International Dateline to the west of Attu so that the date remains that of Alaska.

The water does not freeze in Aleutian harbors—the surrounding seas are too deep for that. Going north from Dutch Harbor on Unalaska Island, one does not encounter sea ice until the shallow water of the northern Bering Sea is reached.

Jim Rearden arrived at Adak from his visit to Kiska aboard an auxiliary-powered sailing schooner which served as a floating base for a camera party. Gear was unloaded at Adak, and the party flew out the next day on a Reeve Aleutian Airway plane. During Jim's stay at Adak, I was privileged to have several long conversations with him.

Traveling as a guest with the camera party was my old friend William Charles House. As a naval petty officer, he commanded the 10–man weather station on Kiska when the Japanese occupied that island on 7 June 1942. House was awakened on that morning by machine gun bullets piercing the walls of their bunkhouse. He and one of his men stayed behind to burn the code books in the radio shack, then fled to the hills. In the clouds on the hilltops he became separated from his men. Subsequently he hid out from the Japanese for 49 days, subsisting on sedges, earthworms, and whatever. Weakness from starvation finally forced him to surrender. Needless to say, Charlie's experience and his hideout were subjects of interest to the camera crews.*

Charlie House's ordeal was only one of the stories discussed with Jim Rearden. Eventually the conversation drifted to the two days of aircraft carrier attacks on Dutch Harbor. Thanks to an elaborate dispersion plan we had developed prior to the attacks, my squadron, VP-42, lost no planes at Dutch Harbor during the raids. Elsewhere, however, we lost three of our twelve squadron planes to the carrier-based Zero fighters. Our sister squadron, VP-41, lost two, I believe. When the Japanese occupied Kiska some three or four days after the carrier attacks on Dutch Harbor, they brought with them, in the *Kimikawa Maru*, Zero float fighters which we code-named "Rufe." A Catalina's (PBY) best defense against either variety of Zero was to get inside a cloud.

Upwards of 30 days after the carrier attack on Dutch Harbor, Bill Thies (Capt. William Thies, USN, ret.), and his crew of VP-41 squadron discovered

---

Author's note: In 1946 House was awarded a bronze star for burning communications ciphers at Kiska while under fire. Admiral Russell sponsored him for the medal.

that the carriers had left behind on its back in an Akutan marsh one of their Zero fighters. The dead pilot was still in it.

This plane was salvaged; repaired at the Naval Air Station, San Diego; and flown in late September 1942. It was the first Zero to be flown in the United States. The knowledge gained in flying this plane was of utmost value in developing tactics to defeat it.

We are delighted that Jim Rearden has undertaken to write the story of the Akutan Zero and its importance in World War II.

JAMES SARGENT RUSSELL,
Admiral, U.S. Navy, ret.

Adm. James Russell retired from active duty in 1965, having served as commander-in-chief, Allied Forces, southern Europe, from 1962.

During World War II he was commanding officer of VP-42, a PBY squadron stationed in the Aleutians. He served as director of military requirements in the Bureau of Aeronautics 1943–44; was a member of Air Technical Intelligence, Supreme Commander, Allied Powers, Japan 1945–46; and was a member of the U.S. Strategic Bombing Survey in Tokyo 1945–46. In 1951 to 1952 he was commanding officer of the USS Coral Sea. In 1955 he became chief of the U.S. Bureau of Aeronautics.

Acknowledgments

Adm. James S. Russell, USN, ret., of Tacoma, sent me off in a quest for information on the Akutan Zero when he teased me with fascinating stories about that airplane upon our first meeting. When he had my appetite fully whetted, he opened his files and library and fed me every scrap of relevant information he had. Further, he spent hours pouring over a draft of my manuscript carefully correcting my abundant errors. His memories of participating in the Aleutian campaign are vivid and detailed and were most valuable in compiling the tiny segment of wartime history that this volume considers.

Rear Adm. William N. Leonard, USN, ret., of Virginia Beach, Virginia, in the words of Barrett Tillman, WWII aviation historian, is a "national treasure" because he is so generous with his time and knowledge, records, and photos. Like Russell, he was a part of history. He fought at the Battle of the Coral Sea, at Midway, at Guadalcanal, and in other major Pacific engagements. Virtually every written source I have consulted about Naval aviation in the Pacific during the first years of the war mentions Leonard somewhere. He, too, spent hours pouring over a draft of my manuscript, carefully correcting errors.

Capt. William N. Thies, USN, ret., of Carmel, California, pilot of the PBY that discovered the Akutan Zero, has likewise been generous with records and photos, in sharing memories, and in opening his home to me and my wife.

Robert C. Mikesh, senior curator of the aeronautics Department of the National Air and Space Museum, Washington, D.C., not only was helpful with information from the museum, he was generous with his personal photos, time, and knowledge.

Comdr. Robert Larson, USNR, ret., of Camano Island, Washington, second pilot of the PBY with Thies when Koga's Zero was found, was most generous in allowing use of his written recollections of the discovery of the downed Zero.

Lt. Gen. Masatake Okumiya, JASDF, ret., patiently provided me with information on the Zero airplane and answered my questions with great courtesy.

Zero ace Saburo Sakai located the family of Tadayoshi Koga to obtain for me biographical information on that 19-year-old pilot who became a footnote to history because he flew the airplane that came to mean so much to the United States.

Ted Spencer, Director of the Alaska Aviation Heritage Museum, Anchorage, was helpful with photos and information pertinent to Aleutian campaign military matters.

The late Guy LaRue, of Eagle River, Alaska, pried out of various government offices many documents relating to the Akutan Zero. His widow Joan generously turned them over to me to use as I wished.

To all of these, and to the dozens of others who have provided bits and pieces of information for this volume, I express my deep appreciation.

Prologue

Wartime, 4 June 1942, Alaska's Aleutian Islands. Three graceful Japanese Zero fighter planes, red "meatballs" on wings and fuselage, flew low over the treeless green island of Akutan, 25 miles east of the American navy base of Dutch Harbor. Behind them rose smoke from the bombing raid in which they had just participated. The pilots of the Zeros sought a landing place for one of the planes that had been crippled by gunfire.

At a grassy, level valley floor half a mile inland, Flight Petty Officer Tadayoshi Koga, an unsmiling, rather small and quiet 19-year old, reduced throttle and held up the nose of his crippled Zero until his speed dropped to 80 mph; he then lowered wheels and flaps and guided the plane to a three-point landing. As he flared and the wheels touched, the Zero flipped onto its back, tossing into the air water and gobs of mud. The grassy flat was a bog.

The remaining Zeros, flown by Chief Petty Officer Endo and Flight Petty Officer Tsuguo Shikada, circled. There was no movement at the downed plane. If Koga was dead they knew they must try to destroy the downed Zero. They had enough ammunition; a few incendiaries would do it.

In the end they couldn't make themselves shoot. Perhaps Koga would recover, destroy the plane himself, and make his way to the beach where a Japanese submarine waited to pick up stray pilots. Low on fuel, Endo and Shikada set course for the aircraft carrier *Ryujo* 200 miles to the south, from which they had flown for the attack on Dutch Harbor.

Five weeks later the Zero with Koga's body still in it was spotted from a patrolling American airplane. Koga's Zero, often called the Akutan Zero or the Aleutian Zero, was a prize almost beyond value to the United States, then in the sixth month of its 46-month war with Japan. So far the mysterious Zero fighter had outflown every fighter plane that the Allies had thrown against it.

This is the story of Koga's Zero and what it meant to the United States at war.

one

An Aerodynamic Impossibility

In 1937 Japan was involved in war with China, and Japan was the aggressor. For the previous quarter of a century Japan had developed her naval air power, importing European and American warplanes for evaluation while developing her own military planes. The new Japanese planes had been kept within Japan, unseen by prying foreign eyes. As a result, the outside world had little idea of the strength of Japanese naval aviation.

In the fall of 1937 Japanese Type 96 twin-engine, twin-rudder bombers, later code-named "Nells" by the U.S., flew farther on transoceanic missions than had any other nation's planes. (Japanese warplane designations were confusing to Americans. To simplify identification, WWII Japanese bombers were given anglicized feminine names by the Allies, while fighters were given masculine names.)

Japanese raids on China occurred day and night, in good weather and bad, from Formosa and from Japan's Kyushu Island, with round trip flights averaging more than 1,200 miles.

The Japanese soon learned that bombers were not enough. On 17 August 1937, 12 bombers flew from the aircraft carrier *Kaga* without fighter escort to raid Hangchou. Russian-made fighters flown by Chinese pilots pounced on the raiders and shot down all but one. The 12th bullet-riddled plane flown by Lt. (jg) Minoro Tanaka, staggered back to the *Kaga*. Japanese tacticians were amazed by Tanaka's report of the fighter plane attack.

The Japanese learned that they lost fewer planes when their bombers had fighter escort. That's simple and basic. But it was a new idea then, and the Japanese immediately equipped the *Kaga* with the new Type 96 Mitsubishi (Claude) fighter plane.

The Claude was the world's first operational low-wing monoplane carrier fighter. It was an all-metal, flush-riveted (a new concept then being adopted by American designers), radial-engine plane with fixed gear, designed by a Mitsubishi Company team led by an engineer named Jiro Horikoshi. Horikoshi (1903-1981) was to became famous as designer of the Zero fighter.

The agile and fast Claude fought and bested Chinese pilots flying the English-made Gloster Gladiator, the American Curtiss 75, and the Russian N-15 and N-16 fighters. Robert Short, an American in Shanghai in 1939 delivering a Boeing fighter (probably a P-26), took it up to confront three Claudes. He reportedly lasted about two minutes.

After the appearance of the Claude, Chinese fighter planes essentially disappeared from the air. The Japanese could then bomb when and where they wanted, with only anti-aircraft fire to hinder them.

The Japanese learned a simple but profound lesson from this, a lesson that led almost directly to development of the Zero fighter, and in a way, to Japan's war with the western nations. It became an axiom with the Japanese: He who controls the air, wins the battles.

Subsequent developments reinforced this lesson. By mid-1940 as the war with China dragged on and Chinese defenders retreated and rebuilt their

The Japanese were among the first to realize the potential of naval air power. The *Hosho*, the world's first true aircraft carrier, designed as such from the keel up, was launched by the Japanese in 1922. Small—she was 7,500 tons, could sail at 25 knots, and carried about 20 planes—the *Hosho* was taken off active duty in mid-1942 and used for training. *National Archives.*

The Type 96 Mitsubishi bomber, code-named "Nell" by the U.S., flew farther in 1937 on transoceanic bombing missions than had maximum-range aircraft of any other nation. *National Archives.*

strength, Japanese bombers had to make ever-longer flights. The limited range of the Claude prevented it from escorting the bombers on their long raids—and Chinese pilots again started to down Japanese bombers. The Japanese no longer controlled the air over beleaguered Chinese cities. This was the case until 19 August 1940, when the first 15 Mitsubishi-built Zero fighters appeared in China.

The sleek, long-range Zero fighters escorted 54 Nell bombers. There was no fighter opposition, and the Zeros didn't fire a shot. On that raid, however, the Zero established a new distance record for the combat flight of a fighter by flying a round trip of more than 1,000 nautical miles.

The Mitsubishi A5M Type 96 carrier-borne fighter, code-named "Claude" by the U.S., was the world's first operational low-wing monoplane carrier fighter. It was highly successful. Jiro Horikoshi, its designer, became famous as designer of the Mitsubishi Zero fighter. *National Archives.*

On 13 September, 13 Zeros escorted a flight of Nells that bombed Chungking. Chinese intelligence had warned their fighter pilots against tangling with the Zero. After the bombing, the Japanese planes left behind a high-flying reconnaissance plane. The pilot of that plane soon radioed that Chinese fighters were in the air over Chungking.

The Zeros returned and dived out of the sun to attack 27 Russian-made N-15 and N-16 fighters. Shortly, all 27 planes had been downed. Two crashed into mountains as they fled the Zeros, and three Chinese pilots, after seeing their companions shot down, bailed out of their untouched fighters. Four Zeros were damaged, none lost.

Flight Warrant Officer Koshiro Yamashita became an ace by shooting down five of the Chinese planes. After that, the Zero dominated the skies of China; the Chinese pilots in their outmoded fighters didn't have a chance.

Overall in China in 1940, Zeros flew 70 raids, shot down 99 planes, with 4 probables, while damaging 163 others. Only 2 Zeros were lost, both to anti-aircraft fire, while 39 were damaged.

Claire Chennault, a retired U.S. Army officer advisor to China's leader Chiang Kai-shek and later commander of the American Volunteer Group (AVG)—better known as the Flying Tigers—sent a report to Washington in the fall of 1940 with photos of the Zero and estimates of its performance. The U.S. War Department's response? "Bunk. Such an airplane is an aerodynamic impossibility."

One military man who didn't ignore intelligence reports on Japan's mysterious Zero fighter plane was John Smith "Jimmy" Thach, a 1927 graduate of the U.S. Naval Academy, an aerial gunnery expert, and a test pilot for experimental navy aircraft. Legendary as a leader, he carved a distinguished career for himself during WWII, both flying against the Japanese and directing carrier-based fighters. He retired as a four-star admiral in 1967 and died in 1981.

Rear Adm. William N. Leonard, USN, ret., now of Virginia Beach, Virginia, served with Thach during WWII. In 1988 he described Thach to me as tall, spare but muscular, with a great sense of humor. He was all business, meticulous, and deadly serious, however, on matters of naval aviation, particularly carrier fighters.

A Fleet Air Tactical Unit bulletin describing a new Japanese carrier fighter reached Thach in the fall of 1941 when his Fighting Three Squadron was at the Naval Air Station, San Diego. If the figures were to be believed, the airplane could outfly any U.S. Navy plane. It reportedly climbed at 3,500 feet or more per minute, had high speed, and was incredibly agile. Thach theorized that if the mysterious Japanese plane were only half as good as reported, it was still as capable as the Grumman F4F-3 Wildcat, the Navy's newest fighter.

As Thach and other U.S. Navy pilots subsequently learned, the early model Zero actually had a climb rate of about 2,750 feet per minute. At low to moderate speeds, even at the end of WWII, any model Zero (the plane was modified and improved throughout the war) could turn inside any other fighter plane, and it flew faster than many 1941 U.S. fighters. From a performance standpoint in 1941, it was the finest aircraft carrier fighter in the world.

Since war with Japan appeared likely, Thach decided to prepare for encounters with the supposed super fighter. U.S. Navy fighter planes had excellent guns and pilots who could shoot well. Thach decided to devise a way to give U.S. planes a chance to use these strengths against the reported new Japanese plane. In the summer of 1941 he worked on the problem at night at his home in Coronado, California, using kitchen matches to represent airplanes, experimenting with different formations and different maneuvers, imagining in three dimensions. Next day he tried his ideas aloft.

Throughout the 1930s most of the world's military planes flew formation in three-plane sections, with a leader and two wingmen. This is awkward for abrupt maneuvering. One wingman might follow the leader, but the second was often in the way. In July 1941 the U.S. Navy changed to two-plane sections, and this change fit Thach's ideas.

Thach concluded that a two-plane section using a four-plane division or combat unit could cope with the reported Japanese super plane. Eventually he settled on having the two pairs of planes fly a distance apart equal to the tightest half circle the airplanes involved could turn. With such a formation, if an enemy plane came from directly ahead, one plane could get a head-on shot, while the other could turn into the enemy to get a deflection or crossing shot. But what if the enemy were astern? A pilot can't see directly behind, and

Lt. Cmdr. John "Jimmy" Thach, probably in 1942. He gained fame as a fighter pilot during WWII, successfully meeting the Japanese in the Grumman Hellcat fighter. The Thach weave, developed before the war by Thach, helped Wildcat pilots defeat the Zero in combat. Thach retired from the Navy as a four star admiral in 1967 and died in 1981. *National Archives.*

spotting a plane diving from the rear or approaching from behind is virtually impossible.

Thach and his squadron discovered, as they experimented with the new concept, that if the pilot of a two-plane formation on the right watched over the tail of the plane on his left, while the pilot on the left watched over the tail of the plane on his right, aircraft approaching from the rear could be handled. A pilot had to have confidence in his wing-mate, but it worked.

If you were flying on the left side of the formation you didn't have to worry about watching to your left and rear, because the guy on the right was doing that. And vice versa.

The signal that an enemy plane was near lethal range on your tail was a sharp turn toward you (and the enemy plane) by your wingmate, who was out there half a turning circle away. At that signal—a sharp turn of your wingmate toward you—you also turned sharply, throwing off the enemy's aim. Your wingmate came around and got a shot at the enemy, who by then would be trying to correct his original course to get his sights back on your plane.

Thach and his squadron used their Brewster F2A Buffaloes as "Zeros" and "U.S. Planes," using half power with the "U.S. Planes," and allowing the attacking "Zeros" to use full power, thus giving the "Zeros," or attacking planes, much better performance.

The "Zeros" attacked from front and behind, overhead, below, one side or the other. Every time a "Zero" lined up to shoot at a low-performance "U.S. Plane," the "U.S. Plane" would weave out of the way, and a wingmate would, for a moment at least, line his guns up on the attacking "Zero." The maneuver came to be called the Thach Weave. When war came, it gave the Grumman F4F Wildcat the margin it needed to cope with the more agile Zero.

From beginning to end of WWII, that "aerodynamic impossibility," the Zero fighter, all too often shot down our fighters and bombers alike. Near war's end, bomb-laden Zeros even threatened our major combat ships, for it was the main airplane used by kamikaze or suicide pilots.

For U.S. aviators, and for those who were responsible for designing and producing their aircraft, the mystery was where the Zero had come from.

two

Designing the Zero

Early in WWII, U.S. aviation experts believed that the Zero fighter plane was a copy or a modification of an American or a European design, and that the Japanese were incapable of building an airplane with performance superior to U.S. planes. The truth is, the Zero was as much Japanese design as any airplane of the day could be.

The Zero was built in response to a need. To win modern (1930s) wars, control of the sky was essential. The Mitsubishi Claude fighter proved that in China. Long-range bombers soon outdistanced the Claude, and the Japanese realized they needed a fighter with longer range, among other attributes.

The Imperial Japanese Navy Air Staff decided they needed a carrier-borne fighter that could:

- intercept and destroy attacking enemy bombers
- escort Japanese bombers on missions
- have combat performance greater than that of any potential enemy interceptor.

In May 1937 the Navy Air Staff established specifications for the new fighter, which was to enter combat in three years. The specs described an airplane advanced over anything then flying.

It was expected to:

- fly at 310 mph at 13,123 feet
- climb to 9,843 feet in 3½ minutes
- fly at maximum continuous power at 9,843 feet fully loaded with auxiliary fuel tank for 1.5 to 2 hours
- land at less than 67 mph
- take off in 230 feet into a 30 mph wind; or in 574 feet in calm air
- be fully instrumented and radio-equipped, including radio homer
- be equipped with oxygen and fire extinguisher
- be armed with two 7.7mm machine guns and two 20mm cannon
- be as maneuverable as the A5M Mitsubishi (Claude) fighter then in use
- have a wing span of less than 39 feet 4 inches (12 meters) in order to fit the elevators used on aircraft carriers

Mitsubishi engineer Jiro Horikoshi, who had designed the A5M Claude, headed the Mitsubishi design team. Lightness, simplicity, and ease of maintenance were the main elements of the design philosophy.

It was clear that the new fighter would have to be exceedingly light. No armor was included, nor were self-sealing fuel tanks. Steel forgings were reduced in size or eliminated. The wing was integral with the center section of the fuselage, thus doing away with the heavy fittings needed for attaching wings to fuselage. The fuselage separated behind the trailing edge of the wing where two fuselage rings bolted together, making it possible to easily get at the cockpit for repairs.

The light weight and good design produced a plane that responded easily to the slightest control movement, and nimbleness became the Zero's trademark. The Zero's vulnerability—hits in the unprotected pilot or the fuel tanks—was the other side of that coin.

A new lightweight Extra-Super Duralumin (ESD) was used as a main part of the wing spar, the main strength component of a wing. I-shaped, the flange or top segment of the spar formed part of the wing surface, with the skin riveted to the flange, thus saving a few pounds.

Despite the large-diameter 950-hp Nakajima Sakae 12 radial engine used, the Zero had one of the slimmest silhouettes of any WWII fighter. There were no bulges to give parasitic drag. A glance at a photo of the front view of an airborne Zero makes one wonder where the big 14-cylinder engine is. The two rows of seven cylinders were of very snug proportions, with elongated reduction gear housing and a long shaft that put the engine deep in the fuselage behind the propeller. It had very good aerodynamics. The smooth flowing and graceful lines show clearly, and the pronounced wing dihedral added to the lovely symmetry of the airplane.

The fuselage and canopy appear longer than necessary, but this feature added to flight stability, while emphasizing the long smooth lines. The 12-meter wingspan and light weight (about 5,500 pounds with fuel, ammunition, and pilot) gave it a very low wing-loading (area of wing in relation to weight). Large ailerons gave it great maneuverability at low speeds.

At 230 mph, the Zero could reverse direction 180 degrees in less than six seconds, losing only about 40 mph in speed and traveling less than 1200 feet forward.

The first model Zero was completed at the Mitsubishi factory in southern Nagoya. To test-fly the new plane, it had to be disassembled and hauled 25 miles to the nearest suitable airfield on ox-drawn wagons. This hints at the primitive/modern traits of the Japan that was about to bring war to the West. At this airfield Mitsubishi's test pilot Katsuzo Shima briefly lifted the prototype off the runway for the first time in a jump-flight in April 1939.

The original two-blade propeller was replaced with a three-blade constant speed prop—the first one to be used on a Japanese-made plane. The retractable landing gear gave problems, and hard landings sometimes caused landing gear failure. Another persistent problem was the occasional failure of

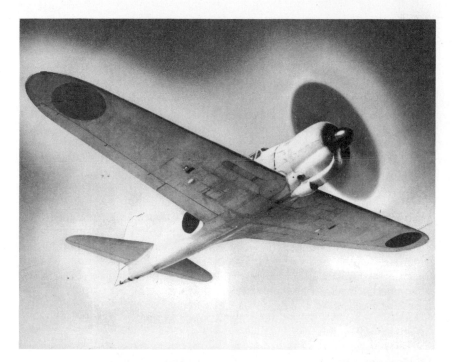

An early model (Model 21) of the A6M Mitsubishi Zero. Allies code-named it "Zeke," but Zero and Zeke were used interchangeably. *Robert C. Mikesh.*

the release for the auxiliary gas (belly) tank; pilots sometimes had to dogfight with the tank still attached.

The Zero was accepted by the Japanese Navy in July 1940 and designated A6M1 Type 0 Carrier-borne Fighter. The 0 came from the last number of the Japanese calendar year when the airplane was put into service—2600: 1940 in the Western calendar. In Japanese it was *Rei Shiki Sento Ki* (Type Zero Fighter), sometimes shortened to *Rei-sen* or *Reisen.* To many Japanese it was *Zero-sen.*

The Allied military designation for the airplane during WWII was Zeke. But Zero was already known, and the two names were used interchangeably. The float-equipped Zero, which fought in the Aleutian and Solomon Islands, was code-named Rufe.

How much did the design of the Zero owe to American or European airplane design? A question of the same ilk today might be, What design features have Japanese automobile engineers borrowed from American and European engineers?

Clearly, there is a pool of worldwide information in all fields from which engineers freely draw. When Horikoshi designed the Zero, he used both American and European aircraft design knowledge, plus his own knowledge and skill.

We were at peace with Japan when the first Zeros were built, and some Zero components were built under license from U.S. manufacturers, such as wheels and instruments from Bendix and propellers under license from Hamilton Standard. The Oerlikon 20mm cannon used in the Zero was built under license from Oerlikon of Switzerland. In wartime, many aircraft components used by the Japanese were direct copies of American designs—such as those from Sperry, Kollsman, and others. The Zero's retractable landing gear was probably a modification of that used in the U.S.-built Vought 143 fighter, an example of which the Japanese bought in 1937.

The Zero was unique in being the lightest and most agile of all major WWII fighters. It could even outmaneuver the famed British Spitfire. This brought many benefits, but the light weight of the Zero was possible because of measures taken to reduce its weight, such as eliminating pilot-protecting armor and self-sealing fuel tanks. This made the pilot and fuel tanks vulnerable; the Zero was often brought down by strikes that could be shrugged off by armored and self-sealing-tank-equipped American fighter planes. Without the self-sealing feature, the Zero was easily flamed when hit in any one of its three fuel tanks. The Zero was probably the easiest of any WWII fighter to bring down when hit.

Who could be a better authority on the Zero than a Japanese naval aviation officer from WWII? In October 1986 Masatake Okumiya was a guest of honor of the Alaska Historical Society at Anchorage for the premier showing of the film "Alaska at War."

Okumiya, then 77 years old, 5 feet tall, and only 95 pounds, still carried himself in erect military bearing. His face had burn scars from the crash of a dive bomber he was test-flying about 1940; it caught fire in flight. Okumiya survived more air-sea battles during the war than any other Japanese. In June 1942 he was flight operations officer aboard the carrier *Ryujo* when its planes attacked Dutch Harbor.

With Jiro Horikoshi, designer of the Zero, Masatake Okumiya wrote the book *Zero*, praised by some U.S. authorities as one of the best books ever written on Japanese naval aviation during WWII.

I asked Okumiya what he considered to be the greatest weakness of the Zero.

"No armor," was his succinct answer.

On the positive side, one trait of the Zero that the Japanese exploited was its tremendously long "legs." The Imperial Navy Air Staff wanted a long range fighter, but even they had no idea of the long range wonder that would be created from their specifications.

Long before the attack on Pearl Harbor, Japanese war planes were concentrated at Formosa with the idea of attacking the Philippines. It is 450 nautical miles from Formosa to Clark Air Base and Iba Fields on Luzon, where most American air power in the Philippines was located in 1941. Those two airfields, plus the city of Manila, 500 nautical miles from Formosa, were considered critical war targets by the Japanese.

In October 1940, the Japanese stationed the aircraft carriers *Zuiho*, *Ryujo*, and *Kasuga-Maru* at Formosa to train Zero pilots for an attack on the Philippines. In the initial bombing, the Zeros were to fly from Formosa to the carriers, which were to be stationed near Luzon, refuel, and then fly on, escorting bombers to Clark and Iba fields. Afterward the Zeros would fly directly back to Formosa.

The pilots were urged to extend the range of their Zeros. This they did to an amazing degree. Normal fuel consumption was about 35 gallons an hour. With a load of 182 gallons, that gave a flight endurance of about five hours.

Experimenting, the pilots learned they could coax the Zero into sipping minimal fuel by flying at 12,000 feet and loafing along at 115 knots, with the fuel-air mixture at its leanest setting. Eventually Zeros were remaining aloft in mass formation for an amazing 12 hours. Saburo Sakai, famed at the end of the war as Japan's leading surviving fighter ace, established a Formosa-training low-fuel consumption record of less than 17 gallons an hour.

When, months into the war, U.S. experts learned of the fantastic range of the Zero, they considered it one of the wonders of the aviation world. No fighter plane had ever before flown such distant combat missions. The British Spitfire and the German Me 109, leading European land-based fighters of the time, had ranges of less than 600 miles with auxiliary tanks. The main U.S. Navy fighter of the time, the Grumman Wildcat (F4F), had a combat radius of about 200 miles and a nominal range of 800 or so miles. The way the Zero could appear suddenly as if from an aircraft carrier, when it had actually flown from distant land bases, gave it an aura of mystery.

The confidence of the Japanese in the ability of the Zero to dominate the skies wherever it appeared was an important element in the decision of the Japanese to bring war to the West. In 1941, some Japanese military experts believed one Zero was the equal of from two to five enemy fighters. This confidence was not, in the beginning at least, misplaced.

three

The Long-Lived Zero

The Zero was Japan's main fighter plane throughout WWII. In 1940 and 1941, from a flight performance standpoint, it was the finest carrier-based fighter in the world. By war's end Mitsubishi had built 3,830 Zeros, and Nakajima had built 6,750, for a total of 10,580. Additionally, Nakajima built 323 Rufes—Zero floatplanes—and the 21st Naval Air Depot and Hitachi Aircraft Company built 517 two-seat Zero trainers.

The Japanese depended heavily on the Zero, and during the war they were not prepared to or weren't capable of building more advanced fighters in the numbers needed to cope with increasing numbers and quality of U.S. fighters. At war's end about half of all Japanese fighter planes were Zeros, little changed from the Zero that had first fought in China five years earlier.

On 7 December 1941, it dominated the skies at Pearl Harbor, as the Japanese had planned. It also essentially cleared Philippine skies of American fighters within days of the attack on Pearl Harbor, flying the 450 nautical miles from Formosa to accomplish this.

Without the Zero, however, the Japanese had a difficult time taking Wake Island. U.S. defenders threw back the first attempt at landing on 11 December 1941. A dozen Grumman Wildcats controlled the skies instead. The first Japanese raid wrecked seven of them. By the last day there were only two Wildcats left. They earned their keep. These rugged little planes even sank a Japanese destroyer and damaged a couple of light cruisers. But on 23 December when the carriers *Soryu* and *Hiryu* arrived with their Zeros, the two remaining Wildcats were quickly shot down, and Wake fell.

On 24 December the Japanese seized tiny Jalo Island in the southern Philippines and immediately flew 24 Zeros there from Formosa, a distance of 1,200 miles. This was an unprecedented flight for a single-seat fighter.

Early in the war, the Zero scored heavily. As planned, it controlled the skies wherever it appeared. Port Darwin, Australia, for example, was attacked

Lt. William N. Leonard, 10 March 1949, in a FH-1 jet aboard the carrier *F.D. Roosevelt.* Leonard fought in the Gilberts, at the Battle of the Coral Sea, at Midway, Guadalcanal, in the Philippines, in Indochina and Okinawa-Taiwan, and in the Japanese home islands. He served aboard the carriers *Yorktown, Wasp, Hancock,* and *Shangri-La.* When he retired as a rear admiral in 1971 he was qualified to fly more than 50 types of aircraft, including jets. Among the various aircraft he flew was the Akutan Zero. *National Archives.*

on 19 February 1942 by 190 Japanese planes. Zeros shot down the eight defending Australian fighters.

Colombo, Ceylon, was attacked by 36 Zeros and 89 bombers on 27 March. About 60 British fighters rose to defend, but Zeros shot down almost all of them with scant loss to themselves.

Trincomalee, Ceylon, was attacked by Japanese planes on 9 April 1942. Zeros shot down 56 defending British fighters, including 10 Hawker Hurricanes, which had become famous against Hitler's Luftwaffe during the Battle of Britain. British Blenheims attempted to bomb the raiding Japanese carriers, but Zeros shot down all nine.

It was 7 May 1942 before a U.S. Navy pilot downed a Zero. Rear Adm. William N. Leonard, USN, ret., who ended the war as an ace with six Japanese planes—including two Zeros—to his credit, has provided a perspective of the time.

In a letter to me he wrote, "My *Yorktown* squadron VF-42's first Zero encounter occurred in the Battle of the Coral Sea on 7 May 1942. This was during the strike on the small Japanese carrier *Shoho*, which based a few Zeros. VF-42 pilot, Lt. (jg) Walt Haas, is credited with shooting down a strange machine that could outspeed the F4F-3 Grumman Wildcat."

The record shows that Haas saw the enemy plane flying in his direction, chased by another Wildcat. Haas dived, trading altitude for speed, and when in range he fired on it from behind. The Zero tried a steep climbing turn. Haas fired again, setting it aflame. It dived into the water. Its pilot was probably Warrant Officer Shigemune Imamura, a veteran of aerial fighting in China.

More from Leonard: "At that time we had no way of identifying the plane Haas shot down as a Zero. We encountered more of these strangers the next day and still did not know what to call them. Some were even misidentified as German Messerschmitt 109s. As more information came in we realized we were fighting a thing called Zero. In these encounters and on our own we were learning the folly of dog fighting with this new-to-us airplane and the merits of high-speed and altitude advantage if we could get it.

"From the way the Zero pilots rollicked about the sky, at times it looked as though they would rather stunt than fight. That would be a great temptation in a machine that handled like the Zero I flew." (See Chapter 10.)

In the tragic victory of Midway, Zeros slaughtered American torpedo bombers and their crews. Luck and the sacrifice of the lives of scores of young Americans brought the U.S. a miraculous victory.

During the Battle of Guadalcanal, the superior firepower, teamwork, flying, and shooting skill of U.S. pilots saw the Japanese and their Zeros losing dominance in the Pacific. The Japanese lost 600 planes during the six-month campaign. They had lost many of their top pilots and aircraft crews at Midway, and the grinder of Guadalcanal continued this process. At the same time the U.S. was gaining in numbers of pilots and planes, and its planes were improving by leaps and bounds.

The Zeros had to fly 560 nautical miles from Rabaul and return in order to escort bombers and attack Guadalcanal. This stretched even the great range of the Zero. Pilots of the Zero had to fly, and sometimes dogfight, with belly tanks handicapping them.

Bill Lindley, now 73, a slim, straight-backed six-footer who winters in Yuma, Arizona, and summers at Madras, Oregon, has vivid memories of three Zeros he once encountered in the skies near Guadalcanal. Lindley retired from the U.S. Marine Corps in 1967 after 30 years of service. Originally he was an NAP (enlisted pilot). He was promoted to Chief Warrant Officer while flying at Guadalcanal in 1942.

In January 1988 Lindley described to me his encounter with the Zeros. "I was flying an SBD-3 (Douglas Dauntless dive bomber) at about 8,000 feet, searching for two Jap battleships reported in the area. My gunner was Red Giles who was later killed in action," Lindley recalled.

"Suddenly the corner of my windshield exploded, and a row of bullet holes appeared in my right wing. I went into the steepest climbing turn I could make and at the same time released my two 200-pound bombs.

"Three Zeros had dropped on us out of the sun. Red let fly at the second one with the twin 50s. I think he hit it—that Zero pulled out in an awful hurry.

"Then the third one came in, but I was turning as sharply as I could, and Red fired at him too—and he too pulled out.

"I had no place to hide—there were no clouds anywhere—and I could expect no help. I was all by myself. I figured they had us.

"We had strict orders to not dogfight the Zero. It was suicide. Our orders were to slow down and pull into as tight a climbing turn as we could and outmaneuver them as they came in. With the big flaps on the SBD and full power, we could turn inside a Zero. The idea was to turn so the gunner was looking down their throats.

"After diving on us, the three Zeros pulled off about three-quarters of a mile and circled around us, then they left. I think they blundered into us as they were headed back to Rabaul after escorting bombers to Guadalcanal. They were probably low on fuel and couldn't stay to play with me.

"I was just plain lucky. I caught 14 bullet holes in my wing, and two went through the self-sealing gas tank."

During the fall of 1942 the fast Lockheed Lightning P-38 twin-engine fighter arrived in the Pacific. At first P-38 pilots tried to dogfight the Zero, to the delight of Zero pilots. Later the P-38 pilots turned the tables. With their turbo supercharged engines they could patrol at high altitude, above the height at which the Zero could efficiently fly. They could then plunge from the sky and make a pass at a Zero, continuing to dive until safely beyond reach. Then they would climb to repeat the maneuver if necessary.

The single-engine Chance-Vought F4U Corsair also arrived in the Pacific in the fall of 1942. It was the first single-engine American fighter to outfly the Zero. It was faster than the Zero in level flight, could out-dive it, at higher altitudes outclimb it, and it had far more firepower. The Corsair, however, was a bad actor on carriers—it bounced and had wing-tip stall. These faults were remedied by softening the landing gear oleos (hydraulic shock absorbers) and lengthening the tail wheel strut. The marines at Guadalcanal were glad to get the bouncy early Corsairs, anyway.

In September 1943 the Grumman F6F Hellcat appeared in the Pacific. In the end, this airplane destroyed more Japanese aircraft in the air than any other U.S. plane. The Hellcat could outclimb, outrun, outshoot, and outdive the Zero. It couldn't outturn it.

In November and December 1942 all U.S. fighter pilots in the Pacific eagerly read the results of the test flights of Koga's Zero (see Appendix). The information reinforced and added to what pilots had already learned in the school of hard knocks.

Bill Leonard's comments on the test flight reports: "My squadron VF-11

The F6F Grumman Hellcat destroyed more Japanese aircraft in the air than any other U.S. plane. The Hellcat couldn't outturn the Zero, but it could outclimb, outrun, and outshoot it. Here, an F6F-3 Hellcat gets a take-off wave during the attack on the Marshall Islands, November 1943. *National Archives.*

went west in October '42 and fought in Guadalcanal until the spring of 1943. We were strongly impressed with the intelligence gained by test flights of the Akutan Zero.

"Contrast that information with our situation one year earlier when *Yorktown* and *Lexington* fighters faced the same Zero but had no knowledge how to fight it.

"The Zero's speed, endurance, radius of action, and maneuverability were impressive. Its armament limitations, fragility, and lowering quality of Zero pilots combined to improve our fortunes at 'Cactus' (Guadalcanal). Exploitations of these factors and constant practice of weave tactics and air discipline served my squadron VF-11 very well in the Solomons.

"We remained wary of the Zero, for every once in a while there would be flashes of superior airmanship on the part of the enemy and someone would be hurt. We flew obsolescent F4F-4s there, one of the last squadrons so equipped. All marine VF (fighter squadrons) were in F4U (Corsairs) by May 1943, and the F6F (Hellcat) was only a few months away."

By the fall of 1943, Zero pilots were clearly on the defensive. For example, during the invasion of the Gilbert Islands in November, 12 new Hellcat fighters from the new *Lexington* were on combat air patrol when they were vectored to a formation of 21 Zeros that was approaching the task force.

In a wild battle reminiscent of the Zero-dominated tussles of a few months earlier, but with a reversed outcome, at least 17 of the Zeros were shot down, five by Lt. (jg) Eugene R. Hanks, who thus became the first Hellcat fighter ace in a day.

For 1943 as a whole, U.S. Navy and Marine Corps fighter pilots in Wildcats, Hellcats, and Corsairs shot down 889 single-engine Japanese fighters. Of these, 94 percent were Zeros.

The year 1944 found the Japanese desperate. In the Philippines they turned to kamikaze or suicide pilots who crashed their planes into U.S. flattops at Leyte. At first this was a temporary expedient, but some success led the Japanese to continue with suicide flights. At Okinawa an estimated 1,815 Japanese planes carried out kamikaze attacks on U.S. ships. In April 1944

A kamikaze plane (dark spot in upper center) making a wave-top approach at the port side of the battleship *Missouri* on 11 April 1945. About half of the kamikaze planes were Zeros. *National Archives.*

1,465 kamikaze planes sank 26 American ships and damaged 164 others. Overall there were some 2,393 kamikaze attacks. Of these 1,189 were Zero fighters. The Zero was preferred because its swiftness and maneuverability gave it the best chance of penetrating combat air patrols and crashing into American ships.

John Edward "Big John" Laughton, of Salinas, California, knows about kamikaze Zeros. His memory was still vivid in 1988 when he recalled his horrifying experience for me.

Laughton was second mate aboard the new merchant ship S.S. *Hobbs Victory* carrying 6,000 tons of ammunition destined for the army at Okinawa. On 6 April 1945, the *Hobbs Victory* was anchored in the Kerama Retto, a small group of islands five miles from Okinawa, when suddenly a Zero kamikaze plane crashed into a nearby LST (Landing Ship, Tank). Barrels of fuel oil erupted into an inferno. Within moments a twin-engine Betty flew straight toward the *Hobbs*; gun crews on the *Hobbs* splashed it.

Another Zero kamikaze crashed into the nearby *Logan Victory*, also loaded with ammunition; boats, rafts, and debris blew into the air, but the ammunition didn't explode. Captain Izant of the *Hobbs* ordered his ship underway.

As the ship slowly moved out of the harbor, all guns on the port side opened up on what appeared to be another Zero readying for a run on the ship. As the plane gained altitude its insignia appeared: it was a U.S. Navy Hellcat. Firing ceased, but not before the plane was hit. Its pilot bailed out.

Then a kamikaze Zero, four points off the port bow, roared toward the *Hobbs*, flying 30 or 40 feet above the sea, swinging like the end of a pendulum, trying to evade gunfire from the *Hobbs*. Tracers poured into the Zero, and smoke rolled from the underside of the plane.

The Zero slammed into the *Hobbs* with an unbelievable roar, its bomb exploding. Remnants of the plane crashed through the radio shack, killing the chief radio operator. Concussion knocked everyone to the deck, and some crewmen were blown overboard. Smoke, steam, and fire billowed from the engine room, and fire enveloped the after part of the midship house and number four hatch. The ammunition didn't explode—then. Dazed survivors carried the injured to the two starboard lifeboats, for both portside lifeboats had been shattered by the Zero. Others released life rafts into the water and leaped after them.

The *Hobbs* was still underway. Engine room controls were engulfed by the inferno and were unapproachable; all five crewmen in the engine room had probably been killed instantly.

The lifeboats were launched. Captain Izant, last to leave, dropped from a Jacob's ladder into the sea and was picked up by the motor lifeboat. Thirteen of the crew of 99 died in the attack and subsequent fire.

The *Hobbs* continued underway, a doomed ship afire, without a living crewman on board. At midnight the ammunition in her belly blew in a spectacular sky-reaching explosion. A ship destroyed by a single Zero.

Although the hot new U.S. fighters had abilities that could best the beefed-up Zero models used toward the end of the war (provided they didn't try to turn with them), the Zero, when flown by Japan's best, was still dangerous. (By mid-1944 Zeros had armor protection for pilots and self-sealing tanks.)

On 17 February 1945, U.S. carrier planes twice raided the Tokyo area. Lt. (jg) Sadanori Akamatsu, a Japanese Navy fighter ace flying a Zero from Atsugi, shot down two F6F Hellcats over Tokyo Bay in the morning. That afternoon, during a second U.S. raid, Akamatsu repeated the feat by shooting down two more F6Fs over Atsugi Field.

At war's beginning the Zero seemed unbeatable. Even seven months into the war, little technical information was known about it. Small wonder that naval experts worked so frantically to learn the Zero's secrets once Koga's plane was found.

During WWII, airpower forever changed the way war on land and sea was fought, and the Zero was a major factor in bringing about this revolution. The Zero was a technological triumph, a breakthrough that forced the U.S. into even greater technological breakthroughs.

By 1945 and war's end, the day of the Zero had come and gone. After five years of combat, the relatively unchanged fighter was an outmoded, tired, old warrior, a has–been.

The end of the war and the obsolescence of the Zero could hardly have been anticipated, however, by those U.S. soldiers, sailors, and marines who, in December 1941, first encountered the Zero.

four

The Zero at Pearl Harbor

On 7 December 1941 Bill Lindley, the NAP Marine pilot referred to earlier, was stationed at the Marine Corps Station at Ewa, 10 miles west of Pearl Harbor. He remembers the day well and described it to me in our conversation early in 1988.

"Three of us were near the end of the runway, walking the three blocks from the mess hall back to the barracks after breakfast," he said. "We heard the roar of airplanes and machine guns firing. Suddenly three Zeros flew over, so low we could see the pilots move. Their machine guns sprayed a row of bullets along the street and up the side of a building. We ran for cover. We recognized the planes as Japanese by emblems on wings and fuselage. We didn't know they were Zeros—I had never heard of the Zero.

"More Zeros showed up, and they took turns strafing our planes, which were parked near the runway. I believe we lost 54 aircraft at Ewa that day. All of the damage was from strafing: it set our planes afire. We didn't get a single fighter into the air. I never saw such a confused mess in my life. We were caught flat-footed."

"The Hawaiian Operation," the Japanese called it. Its success depended largely on catching the Americans "flat-footed," as Bill Lindley describes it. It was a daring plan, one of the greatest aerial attacks the world has ever seen. Within about two hours Japanese warplanes destroyed one of the most powerful battleship fleets in the world. It also thrust the United States and Japan into an aircraft carrier war.

The Japanese based their attack plan on the premise that the Zero could control the skies, allowing bombers and torpedo planes to drop explosives at will. Although the bombs and torpedoes wrought most of the destruction, it was the Zero that made it all possible, and strafing Zeros played a major part in wrecking U.S. air power on Oahu.

On 25 November (Hawaiian date), the powerful 31–ship Japanese armada slipped out of the remote Kurile Islands to sail a great arc toward the Aleutian Islands, then south to Hawaii. It was under the command of Vice

The Nakajima B5N Type 97, code-named "Kate," a three-man monoplane bomber, was capable of carrying either bombs or torpedoes. Kate bombers, flown from carriers, attacked Pearl Harbor as well as Dutch Harbor. *National Archives.*

Adm. Chuichi Nagumo, 54, an old-line naval officer who knew torpedoes, battleships, and cruisers. The armada took a lonely route traveled by few ships, and rough seas and bad weather were the rule. Aboard the carriers *Akagi, Kaga, Soryu, Hiryu, Shokaku,* and *Zuikaku,* were 423 planes, of which 350 would attack the greatest American stronghold in the Pacific.

Aboard, of course, was the ubiquitous Zero. Included, too, were the Nakajima B5N Type 97 (later code-named "Kate" by the U.S.), a three-man low-wing monoplane with retractable landing gear, capable of carrying bombs for high-level attacks or an aerial torpedo; and the Aichi D3A (Val), a low-wing monoplane two-man dive bomber with fixed-gear, capable of carrying a bomb load of 816 pounds.

Naval aviation was new to Nagumo. Although he was opposed to the attack on Hawaii, seniority had given him this command. With his opposition and the burden of responsiblity weighing heavily on his shoulders, Nagumo was a great contrast to his crew. Most of his airmen were young and enthusiastic. They harbored modern ideas and had great faith in the striking power of modern aircraft.

On 6 December Nagumo's ships were about 600 miles north and west of Oahu when they increased speed to 20 knots for a final overnight dash to get within striking distance.

The night was black and the sea rough. Planes for the first wave were lined up on flight decks; those for the second wave were on hanger decks. Pilots wrote farewell letters home then tossed restlessly in their bunks. Lt. Fusata Iida, 27, a Zero squadron leader on *Soryu*, had been among the first to fly the Zero in China. He declared, "If I have engine trouble, I will crash into an enemy target rather than make an emergency landing."

Prophetic words.

At dawn, two float-equipped Zeros (Rufes) were catapulted from the heavy cruisers *Chikuma* and *Tone*. They were to radio back information on where the American warships were anchored.

At 5:50 A.M., the six carriers swung into the east wind and increased speed to 24 knots in order to launch aircraft.

Comdr. Shigeru Itaya, who had trained the Zero pilots for the raid, left the *Akagi* first, flying a Zero. His plane passed the bow, engine roaring, flaps

A Kate seen at the Experimental Aircraft Association fly-in at Oshkosh, Wisconsin, in July 1988. This could be a replica, although if it is, it's a good one. *Author photo.*

The Aichi D3A low-wing monoplane fixed-gear dive bomber (code-named "Val") could carry a bomb weighing 816 pounds. Attacks on Pearl Harbor by these bombers were devastating. *National Archives.*

down, to disappear from sight. Then it reappeared, gaining speed as it climbed above the fleet, blue-green (starboard) and red (port) navigation lights on for guidance of the other planes.

Within 15 minutes, 183 warplanes roared from the decks of the six pitching carriers—43 Zeros, 49 Kate horizontal bombers, 51 Val dive bombers, and 40 Kates carrying torpedoes. One Zero splashed into the sea on takeoff; a destroyer rescued the pilot.

The ships turned south as soon as the last plane was off, edging closer to Oahu while crews readied the second wave for takeoff.

Just after 7:00 A.M. the fleet again turned into the east wind and increased speed. Again the Zeros—36 of them this time—flew off first, followed by 54 Kate horizontal bombers, and 77 Vals.

The Japanese planes were beautiful in flight, their massed wings shining in the tropical sky. The Zeros cruised easily, engines throttled back, mixture lean, as they loafed along at 14,100 feet, guarding the Kates and Vals that flew below.

The mastermind of the strike, Lt. Comdr. Mitsuo Fuchida, aboard one of the Kates, tuned to Honolulu radio station KGMB and listened to the Hawaiian melodies that poured out. The needle of his homing radio receiver obediently pointed out the heading to KGMB's transmitter.

The Rufe float Zero from the cruiser *Chikuma*, flew high over Pearl Harbor, unnoticed by any American. It reported that nine battleships, one heavy cruiser, and six light cruisers were in Pearl Harbor (there were actually eight battleships; the pilot counted the target ship *Utah* as a battleship). A few minutes later he radioed a weather report.

Commander Fuchida's plane reached Barber's Point. No anti-aircraft fire greeted him. No fighter plane rose in defense. He radioed the code words *Tora! Tora! Tora!* (Tiger! Tiger! Tiger!), which told the listening Japanese fleet that the Americans had been caught with their pants down. That calm, lovely, warm tropical Sunday morning was then shattered by the roar of diving planes and explosions, and clouds of black smoke rose as bombs and torpedoes hit their targets.

A Val seen at the Experimental Aircraft Association fly-in at Oshkosh, Wisconsin, in July 1988. This could be a replica. *Author photo.*

Twenty-five Vals screamed out of the sky to drop bombs amidst Curtiss P-40 fighter planes parked wingtip-to-wingtip at the Army's Wheeler Field. This virtually wiped out the possibility of significant fighter opposition. Wheeler Field became a sea of fire. Strafing Zeros followed the bombers, destroying every possible plane, shredding buildings, trucks, and autos with fire from their two wing-mounted 20mm cannon and the pair of cowl-mounted 7.7mm machines. The two sets of guns could be fired separately or together. Flames spread from plane to plane, fueled by aviation gasoline. When the attack was over there were more than 40 burned and bullet-riddled fighters at bomb-pocked Wheeler.

At the same time, 26 Vals roared down on Hickam Field, the Army bomber base just south of Pearl Harbor. Some of these Vals diverted to attack targets on Ford Island, in mid-Pearl Harbor.

The attacking planes, especially the first wave, had plenty of time to bomb, torpedo, and strafe, with minimum opposition.

U.S. Navy Lt. Comdr. Logan Ramsey, in the operations center on Ford

A Curtiss P-40 Warhawk fighter taking off from a carrier. The P-40 was the primary Army fighter at the outbreak of WWII. It could outdive the Zero, but was outclassed otherwise. On 7 December 1941 most of the P-40s at Pearl Harbor were destroyed on the ground. *National Archives.*

A newly arrived Army B-17 Flying Fortress destroyed on a runway of Hickam Field during the 7 December 1941 Japanese attack. *National Archives.*

Island, was watching out a window as the color guard prepared to hoist the flag. He heard the roar of a diving plane. Momentarily he thought it was a U.S. plane that was in violation of half a dozen safety rules. When the bomb from the plane exploded, however, he ordered all radiomen on duty to transmit in plain English, "AIR RAID, PEARL HARBOR. THIS IS NOT DRILL."

It became one of the most famous radio messages ever.

Eighteen planes from the aircraft carrier *Enterprise*, which was at sea, arrived to land at Ford Island. Zeros shot down four, killing two of the pilots; the other planes somehow landed at the Marine Base at nearby Ewa, or at Ford Island.

Zeros joined the dive bombers in attacking B-17 bombers (Flying Fortresses) parked at Hickam Field. Incendiary bullets flamed many of the Fortresses, and the smoke and fire from burning planes rose in great plumes.

Twelve unarmed B-17 bombers that had flown overnight from California arrived at Oahu. Maj. Truman H. Landon started to land at Hickam when the control tower warned, "You have three Japs on your tail."

Landon landed anyway, and somehow, all of the dozen B-17s managed to put down at various fields around Oahu. Many were holed by Japanese bullets before and after landing, and others were damaged by bombs and strafing after they safely reached the ground.

The first-wave Zeros then flew to the Marine Corps' Ewa Field, and a startled Bill Lindley and his companions saw the machine gun bullets walk down the street and destroy all their planes.

Twenty-one Zeros dived repeatedly on Ewa, machine-gunning and letting fly with their 20mm cannon, destroying parked aircraft. Aviation gas flared, and soon the field was ablaze with burning gasoline and airplanes.

Some Ewa marines yanked a machine gun out of a scout plane and with it shot down one Zero and put bullet holes in others. Some of the Zeros dived so close to the ground on strafing runs that the marines who fired at them with shoulder weapons could scarcely miss.

The Zeros wrecked Wildcats, Douglas Dauntlesses (SBDs), and utility planes. Accounts vary on the number destroyed, from 33 to 47. Bill Lindley's

Burning American warships at Pearl Harbor pour smoke into the air and anti-aircraft fire pocks the sky in this panorama of the Japanese attack photographed from a distant hill. *National Archives*.

memory of the Zeros destroying 54 aircraft at Ewa that day is probably accurate.

U.S. defenders shot down three Zeros, one Val, and five Kates from the first wave. Fuchida, the planner, patrolled high above Pearl Harbor in his Kate as surviving planes of the first wave headed back to their carriers. He then waited for the second wave, to observe its results.

Zeros of the second wave divided into two groups. Sixteen flew to Hickam Field and Ford Island to control the air over the 54 Kate bombers that were assigned to attack these fields. As the bombers approached at 11,000 feet, anti-aircraft fire forced them higher. Their bombs hit two hangers and a mess hall.

Other Zeros of the second wave passed over Kaneohe from the northwest, where they split into two groups. Nine strafed the Kaneohe floatplane installation then flew to Wheeler Field.

Eight or nine Zeros flew to Bellows Field, home of the Eighty-sixth Observation Squadron, a few miles south of Kaneohe where a squadron of P-40s and some observation planes roosted. There Zeros set fire to a fuel truck, damaged two planes, and shot down three planes that American pilots were attempting to get airborne. They also strafed a B-17 that had been among the dozen that had arrived that morning; it had already been wrecked in landing. The second-wave Zeros also sought targets of opportunity, and strafed homes, cars, and people on the streets.

Lieutenant Iida, who had told his fellow pilots that he would dive his Zero into a target if he had engine trouble, dived at the Kaneohe armory. As he did so, a Navy Aviation Ordnanceman named Sands stood, spraddle-legged, firing at the Zero with a Browning Automatic Rifle (BAR). Iida hosed bullets at the sailor, but they slapped the side of the building, leaving Sands untouched.

Iida left to follow other Zeros; then he noticed a spray of gasoline flowing from his plane. Had Sands hit a fuel tank? Iida signaled a fellow pilot, pointing to the spraying gasoline, then to himself, and then to the ground. He circled, closed his canopy, and dived again at the Kaneohe armory, machine guns barking and spattering bullets around the indomitable Sands, who again ignored the bullets and returned fire with his BAR.

The guns of the Zero stopped just before it passed over Sands—Sands' bullets may have killed Iida. The Zero dived vertically into the ground, exploded, and skidded into a dirt bank.

Army lieutenants George S. Welch and Kenneth Taylor from Haleiwa Field had played poker all night at the Wheeler Officer's Club. The game wound up at about the time that Japanese bombs began to fall. They telephoned to order their P-40s readied for combat, then drove to Haleiwa at speeds of 100 mph and took off without orders. They didn't know how many planes were attacking. Ignoring the odds, Welch and Taylor shot down seven Japanese planes—four in their first mission, three in their second.

Other Army Air Force pilots took off in P-40s and obsolescent P-36s. The agile Zeros shot down most of them almost as fast as they got off the ground. The Zeros not only controlled the air, as the Japanese had planned, they helped destroy enough American planes on the ground so that there was little danger of Oahu planes mounting a significant aerial attack on the raiding carriers.

In the interval between waves of attacking planes, U.S. soldiers, sailors and marines managed to get better prepared; six Zeros and 14 dive bombers were shot down from the second wave.

Thus the Japanese lost 29 aircraft (including nine Zeros), and 55 lives (not including nine lost from Japanese midget submarines sunk by the U.S. fleet during the raid)—a small price to pay for tweaking a giant's nose and for toppling the power of that giant, however briefly.

Loss of American lives was tragically high: 2,403 killed, 1,178 wounded. Of the dead, 68 were civilians. Nearly half of all Army, Navy, and Marine Corps aircraft at Oahu was destroyed—188 out of 394.

Seven of eight battleships were sunk or badly crippled. Three cruisers were heavily damaged, as were three destroyers and a number of important support vessels.

The Hawaiian Operation did not fully demonstrate to Americans the flashy combat performance of the Zero, which was seen mostly as it dived and strafed. How can one judge the ability of a fighter by watching it from the ground, flying virtually unopposed? So few U.S. fighters got into the air that little was learned about the dogfighting ability of the Zero—except that it was fast and nimble.

U.S. technical intelligence examined the Zeros shot down at Pearl Harbor. Other than learning what guns they carried, determining that they had no armor protection or self-sealing fuel tanks, and estimating the horsepower of the engines, they couldn't tell much. It was impossible to get performance figures from the piles of wreckage.

David Aiken, American Aviation Historical Society member, Irving, Texas, has made a study of Zero fighters. His records list two Zeros other than those at Pearl Harbor that were downed in the Pacific theater in early months of the war, from which technical information was available.

One of these aircraft, that of Hagime Toshima, crashed on Melville Island after the raid on Darwin, Australia, on 19 February 1942. The forward half of that Zero still exists in a museum near Darwin.

According to Aiken, the next Zero recovered nearly intact by the Allies in the Pacific was that of pilot Maeda Yoshimitsu. This Zero crashed on 28 April 1942 near Cape Rodney, New Guinea. It was repairable and could have been flown, but soldiers sent to recover it blundered when they chopped the wings off, severing the spars.

A model 21 Zero, similar to the Akutan Zero, made a forced landing in late 1942 along the banks of the Yangtze River. It was captured by the Chinese army, was handed over to General Claire Chennault's American Volunteer

Group (Flying Tigers), taken to Kweilin Airfield in southern China, and test flown by U.S. Army pilots.

This Zero was subsequently transported over the hump to India and eventually reached the U.S. Army Research Institute at Wright Field in 1943, long after completion of the test flights of Koga's plane.

As badly as Pacific theater fighter pilots needed specifics on the performance of the Zero, they had to wait until the fall of 1942 for information to be obtained from flights of Koga's Zero.

The role of the Zero in the early stages of World War II can hardly be overestimated. It played a key role in the sneak attack on Pearl Harbor, and

After the Japanese attack at Pearl Harbor, the smashed destroyers *Cassin* (DD 372) and *Downes* (DD 375) lie forward of the battleship *Pennsylvania* (BB 38) in drydock number one. *National Archives.*

without this high-performance fighter, it is unlikely that the attack on Pearl Harbor would ever have taken place.

At Pearl Harbor, the Zeros, Kates, and Vals left behind a smoking and sunken battleship fleet. They also left behind the kind of war that had once been dominated by such dreadnoughts. From the ashes of Pearl Harbor, the U.S. developed a new kind of war, a war of great aircraft carriers and swarms of high-performance airplanes. Over the next four years, the U.S. Navy elevated carrier warfare to a fine art as it cleared the skies of Zeros and other Japanese warplanes and pushed ever closer to the Japanese home islands. This, however, was still in the future. Following Pearl Harbor, the empire of the Rising Sun was on the offensive.

five

The First Raid on Dutch Harbor

Before dawn, 3 June 1942, eight darkened Japanese warships pitched and rolled through the gray North Pacific. Icy water poured across steel decks. The ships were moving inside a great storm which was whooping east toward mainland Alaska. Shivering lookouts peered into the fog, black clouds, and rain squalls, fearing collision with one of their own ships or discovery by American naval units.

The flagship *Ryujo* and her companion, fresh-from-the-shipyard *Junyo*, both light aircraft carriers, had 82 warplanes in their bellies. *Ryujo* was a strange looking carrier, with no island or superstructure cluttering her flight deck. Escorting the flat-tops were the heavy cruisers *Takao* and *Maya*, three destroyers, and a tanker. At dawn they were to launch planes for an attack on the United States Navy base of Dutch Harbor on Unalaska Island.

Unalaska is one of the treeless, volcanic stepping-stone islands of the stormy Aleutian chain that stretches from the Alaska Peninsula across the North Pacific—the world's longest archipelago of small islands. The Aleutians are the American territory nearest the Japanese homeland.

The Japanese were about to expand their war with the United States. The resulting campaign was one about which the eminent naval historian Samuel Eliot Morison wryly commented, "Both sides would have done well to have left the Aleutians to the Aleuts."

During the 15-month Aleutian campaign, violent winds, fog, rain, snow, and ice, more often than not were the most deadly enemy that either side had to face. More aircraft, both American and Japanese, were lost to operational accidents (weather) than in combat. The Japanese lost 69 planes in combat and 200 to the fog and storms. The U.S. and Canada lost a total of 479 planes. Significant to the 11th Air Force was the ratio of total theater aircraft loss to combat loss—6.5 to 1 in the Aleutian theater, compared with a 3 to 1 average for all Pacific theaters.

The Japanese thrust into the Aleutians was partly a sucker move—a diversion. The Japanese thought that the attack would draw U.S. ships from

Pearl Harbor north in a defensive move, thus reducing the number of ships available to defend Midway.

As *Junyo* and *Ryujo* with their consorts pitched through Alaskan waters, the main Japanese fleet was far to the south in warmer climes, headed for Midway Island. When they attacked Midway, the Japanese expected remnants of the American fleet to rush to that island's defense. Then, with the largest and most powerful fleet ever assembled anywhere, the Japanese planned to destroy what American naval power remained in the Pacific.

The scheduled 4 June attack on Midway was the cheese; the lying-in-wait Japanese fleet the trap. The 3 June Dutch Harbor raid was another small hunk of cheese tossed into a corner.

The Japanese hadn't lost a naval battle in 350 years. (The Japanese considered the Battle of the Coral Sea their victory.) They were, therefore, supremely confident. In the Zero they had the finest aircraft carrier fighter plane in the world, and by now the axiom "he who controls the air, wins the battles" was completely ingrained with the Japanese. As a result, the Zero airplane with its remarkable performance had come to represent Japanese

The 10,600 ton light aircraft carrier *Ryujo*, flagship of the fleet that attacked the U.S. Naval base at Dutch Harbor, Alaska, on 3 and 4 June 1942. She carried 48 planes and had no superstructure above the flight deck. From this carrier pilot Koga flew the airplane that came to be known as the Akutan Zero. Planes from the U.S. aircraft carrier *Saratoga* sank the *Ryujo* in August, two months after her raid on Dutch Harbor. *Alaska Aviation Heritage Museum.*

military might. Wherever the Zero had flown, it had controlled the skies.

Although the attack on the Aleutians was a diversion, a thrust to confuse, a hoped-for way to siphon American naval strength north and away from Midway, that wasn't the only Japanese plan for the Aleutians. Lurking to the west of the storm-hidden *Junyo* and *Ryujo* and south of the Aleutians were four cruisers, a screen of submarines, nine destroyers, and three transports carrying 2,500 Japanese army troops.

According to the plan, Adak Island in the mid-Aleutians was to be occupied by Japanese army troops, U.S. military installations there destroyed, and its harbors mined. Why the Japanese selected Adak is obscure, for there were no military installations on Adak, nor did anyone live on that steep and rugged 30-mile-by-20-mile island.

Following the attack on Adak, Japanese troops were then to withdraw from Adak and land on Attu, the most westerly of the Aleutians. At the same time, Japanese Navy landing forces were to occupy Kiska, 200 miles east of Attu—an island with one of the finest harbors in the North Pacific.

Kiska, the Japanese thought, would be a fine base for flying boats which could patrol the northern half of the 1,400 miles between it and Midway. This barrier air patrol would prevent a surprise penetration toward the Empire by U.S. forces in the North Pacific.

When the Japanese got to Kiska they found a fine harbor for ships. A bothersome swell, however, made it less than ideal for the Rufes (float-equipped Zeros) and Mavis four-engine Kawanishi H6K patrol seaplanes that were based there.

The light aircraft carrier *Junyo*, 24,000 tons, was nearly new, with green pilots, when she accompanied the carrier *Ryujo* on the raid on the U.S. Naval Base at Dutch Harbor. *Alaska Aviation Heritage Museum.*

Possession and control of the Aleutians would also, the Japanese reasoned, make further carrier raids of the Doolittle variety more difficult. On 18 April 1942 Col. James Doolittle had led 16 B-25 bombers from the carrier *Hornet* to bomb the Japanese home islands. The astonishing appearance of Doolittle's B-25s over Japan had turned Japanese eyes toward the Aleutians; perhaps long-range bombers could reach Japan from these American islands. The Japanese intended to make sure this didn't happen.

Capt. Tadeo Kato of the *Ryujo*, bundled against the Alaskan cold, remained on the bridge of his pitching ship. He was grimly determined that the attack on Dutch Harbor succeed. But he was also apprehensive. The previous day, *Ryujo* had sailed briefly through a break in the fog and clouds, and at that moment a plane was sighted overhead. It could have been an American PBY (Catalina), a twin-engine long-range amphibian. The plane had disappeared into the mists, and Kato and his boss, Rear Adm. Kakuji Kakuta, the task force commander aboard *Ryujo*, had fretted about it ever since. They had hoped the raid on Dutch Harbor would be a surprise, another Pearl Harbor.

On that 3 June 1942 pilots were awakened at 1:30 A.M. (Tokyo time). Sunrise was at 2:58. The 20 planes that were to fly from *Ryujo* sat on the flight deck, gleaming with moisture, as the chill wind, icy fog, and cold spray whipped past. *Ryujo* led the fleet that had increased speed to 22 knots to carry them through the storm front. Fog blocked the slanting rays of the sun, and the sky looked as black as a winter's night. The temperature was 20 degrees F.

Kakuta turned to Staff Aviation Officer Masatake Okumiya, mastermind for the Aleutian aerial operations. "What do you recommend?"

"Wait for light," Okumiya suggested.

Take-off was delayed.

Pilots feared that they might not find Dutch Harbor, for their maps were based on an incomplete chart that was more than 30 years old. *Ryujo* and *Junyo* broke out of the swiftly moving fog bank into the gray light of the Alaskan June morning, and at 2:45 A.M. (Tokyo time) the order came to launch aircraft. Six Zero fighters were in the front of the mass of parked planes, for they needed less room for takeoff. Each carried two 132-pound bombs.

Ryujo's launching officer swung a green signal lamp and the first Zero pilot gave his plane full throttle and pointed the round nose of his graceful plane down the heaving deck. The take-off was timed so that the Zero would leave the end of the flight deck as it lifted to a wave. The plane slowly rose into the air, aided by the 26-knot speed of *Ryujo* and another 20 knots from the wind she ran into.

The Zero climbed toward the 700-foot ceiling, red and blue-green wing lights on for the benefit of the other planes. The Zeros circled as the 14 Kate bombers slowly left the flight deck, each burdened with a 1,000-pound bomb.

The wave of 46 planes formed up—20 from *Ryujo* and 26 from *Junyo*—and then scattered as low ceiling and turbulence forced them to fly independently. Formation flying was impossible. Alaskan weather was having its way even before the Japanese could drop their bombs.

When all planes had disappeared into the clouds and mist, Kakuta turned his fleet back into the storm to await their return.

The 20 planes from *Ryujo* managed to grope their way to Dutch Harbor. Most of the newly trained pilots of the *Junyo*, however, became lost, and only two of *Junyo*'s planes, both Zeros, reached Dutch. The others considered themselves fortunate to get back to *Junyo* by homing on her radio.

The airplane that had flown over Kakuta's raiding fleet had been, as Kakuta suspected, a patrolling American PBY, and it had spotted the invaders.

Navy code breakers at Honolulu had known the Japanese plans for Midway and the Aleutians for weeks, and search planes had been flying every possible minute. While the U.S. knew the Japanese were going to attack somewhere in the Aleutians, they didn't know where. Since Dutch Harbor was the sole military base the Japanese were thought to know about, that was where the attack was expected. The U.S. even knew that the Japanese planned to send two carriers to the Aleutians.

The U.S. Navy had a veritable spiderweb of search routes. Patrolling PBYs could operate from sea or land, and to insure their safety, they were widely dispersed. Seaplane tenders afforded temporary mobile bases (sea-dromes) at out-of-the-way places where there were no landing fields.

On 3 June squadrons VP-41 and VP-42—originally 24 planes—were searching for the Japanese. They flew out of Sand Point in the Shumagin islands, from Cold Bay's airfield and harbor, from Akutan, from Chernofski Harbor on Unalaska, from the secret airfield at Otter Point on Umnak Island, and from other hidden bays.

The Navy seaplane tender *Gillis*, just departing Dutch at 5:40 A.M. (Alaska time) that 3 June 1942 spotted the bandits on its radar screen at a range of about 10 miles. The *Gillis* warned the base, and air raid sirens screamed.

The gods of weather, however, favored the Japanese. The eye of the storm was just passing Dutch, and visibility from their 10,000 feet altitude was perfect. Sunlight glinted on their wings as the Zeros rolled into screaming dives and each pilot sought targets for his two small bombs. The Kates serenely flew their level-flight bombing runs.

Anti-aircraft fire erupted as soon as the planes appeared. The Japanese were amazed—they had thought their raid would catch the Americans unprepared.

Lt. Jack Litsey (now Lt. Comdr. John F. Litsey, USN, ret., Seattle, Washington) flying mail in his PBY, roared across the bay. Years later his co-pilot, Ralph Morrison (Lt. Comdr. Ralph A. Morrison, USN, ret., also of Seattle) remembered the moment clearly: Zeros attacked the big PBY, and Litsey headed for a nearby spit and beached the plane. One man standing near the radioman was shot through the heart. The radioman received a wound in one hand. Another passenger was wounded, leaped out of the plane, and drowned.

Morrison also abandoned ship, wondering how well his life jacket would work because he had put it on *under* his leather flight jacket. He need not have worried; when he got in the water he found others walking ashore, for the plane had already grounded on the spit.

Another PBY, piloted by Ens. Jim Hildebrand, lifted into the air. His waist gunners poured fire at an attacking Zero, and Hildebrand flew into the clouds, safe.

For 50 minutes Zeros strafed and Kates dropped their bombs. Smoke, fire, dust, and debris rose. The anti-aircraft guns boomed, and small-arms fire rattled as Zeros flew within range. Twenty-five Americans died, and another twenty-five were wounded.

No U.S. fighters challenged. Radio communication with the 70-mile-distant Army Air Force base at Umnak failed. Pilots waiting by their P-40 fighters didn't get word. Other P-40s summoned from 180-mile-distant Cold Bay arrived after the raiders had left.

Two squadrons of PBY Catalina aircraft searched for the Japanese carrier task force that raided the Aleutians in June 1942. This plane was photographed at Dutch Harbor in 1942. The rugged long-range PBYs found and tracked the raiding Japanese and attempted to direct Army bombers into attacking position. *Alaska Aviation Heritage Museum.*

The Japanese flight headed for home. Weather was terrible, and the planes scattered, flying at 100 feet or less through fog, slashing rain, turbulence. All landed safely.

One of the returning pilots spotted four old WWI four-stacker destroyers in Makushin Bay. He radioed the information ahead, and Admiral Kakuta sent fighter planes from *Junyo* and catapulted four reconnaissance seaplanes from the escort cruisers to bomb the old cans.

Junyo's pilots again became lost, and without sighting the destroyers, once more homed on that life-saving radio beacon.

The four seaplanes were not so fortunate. They broke out of the clouds near Umnak Island, site of a secret Army Air Force base. Twenty-one P-40s roared into the air. One of the seaplanes was shot down in flames. The others fled into the fog to find their way back to the cruisers. None of the surviving Japanese pilots knew where the American fighters had flown from.

The day of the first raid on Dutch Harbor ended with the Japanese fleet in the Aleutians unscathed and unlocated. One Japanese reconnaissance plane and pilot had been lost in exchange for 50 dead and injured Americans and some light damage at still-smoking Dutch Harbor.

six

The Zero at Midway

Admiral Yamamoto was certain a Japanese attack on Midway would pull the U.S. fleet from Hawaii in its defense. For the Midway and Aleutians operations he had 350 vessels of all types in eight separate task forces, more than 1,000 warplanes, and more than 100,000 officers and men. He was especially anxious to sink the U.S. aircraft carriers, which had been at sea during the 7 December attack on Pearl Harbor. Japanese confidence was high, for in the Pacific so far their losses had been light and their victories large.

That confidence might not have been so high had they known that the U.S. had solved a key Japanese radio code and knew about the Midway and Aleutian operations.

Adm. Chester Nimitz, commanding the U.S. Pacific Fleet at Pearl Harbor, beefed up Midway's defenses with more men, more firepower, more planes. He then sent nearly the entire remaining U.S. Pacific fleet—three carriers, eight cruisers, 14 destroyers—to lie in wait for Yamamoto's ships.

The big carriers *Hiryu*, *Soryu*, *Akagi*, and *Kaga*, under Vice Admiral Nagumo, with their escort of two battleships, three cruisers, and 11 destroyers, arrived 240 miles northwest of Midway on 4 June, turned into the wind, and launched 36 Kates, 36 Vals, and 36 Zeros to attack Midway.

No sooner were they airborne than another 108 planes of the same mix were readied for another attack. But these Kates were armed with torpedoes and the Vals were loaded with armor-piercing bombs—armament appropriate for attacking ships. Nagumo wanted to be prepared if and when U.S. fleet elements showed up.

PBY pilot Lt. William Chase, patrolling from Midway, first saw the Japanese planes. "MANY PLANES HEADING MIDWAY. BEARING 320, DISTANCE 150," he radioed. Another PBY pilot, Lt. Howard Ady, spotted two of the Japanese carriers. He radioed their course and speed.

Thirty miles from Midway, 20 F2A Brewster Buffalos and seven Grumman F4F Wildcats flown by Marine pilots from Midway attacked the 107

A Brewster Buffalo F2A, as used by the U.S. Marines at Midway, 4 June 1942. The out-dated and outnumbered Buffalos had no chance against the agile Zeros and were quickly shot down. *National Archives.*

Japanese planes. Most of the Marine pilots managed only one attack. The rest of the battle was a shambles; before the Americans could get in a second run, the Zeros were on them. The F4Fs were outclassed, and the outdated Buffalos had no chance whatsoever with the agile Zeros. Seventeen of the U.S. planes were shot down, seven others were seriously damaged, and most of the surviving pilots were injured.

Bombs hit Midway's seaplane hanger, a post exchange, a mess hall, and the powerhouse. Zeros strafed fuel tanks, gun emplacements, trucks, and small boats. The strike was successful, and Japanese losses light—postwar Japanese records listed losses as two Kates, one Val, and two Zeros. As the attackers headed home, Lt. Joichi Tomonaga, leader of the flight, radioed that a second strike was necessary.

Shortly, six brand new Navy TBFs (Grumman Avenger torpedo bombers), a detached part of the aircraft carrier *Hornet*'s Torpedo Squadron 8 that was stationed temporarily at Midway, attacked the Japanese carriers. It was the first action for the TBF. Zeros from the combat patrol shot down five of them almost immediately, and only one of the squat slow planes staggered back to Midway, bomb doors open, one wheel dangling, one dead gunner on board, the other gunner wounded. The hydraulics had been shot out and control cables severed, and the pilot, with shrapnel in his jaw, had to use the trim tabs for longitudinal control.

Four Army B-26 twin-engine Marauder bombers from Midway attacked the Japanese carriers. A horde of Zeros swarmed over them. The Zeros continued to attack as the bombers flew through heavy anti-aircraft fire to launch torpedoes. Only two of the B-26s returned to Midway. The carriers were untouched.

The American attacks had both come from the direction of Midway, convincing Nagumo that they were shore-based and that no U.S. fleet elements lurked nearby. It also persuaded him to ready for a second attack on Midway.

At 7:15 A.M. he ordered his second-wave planes to be suitably re-armed for another attack on Midway. This meant that the torpedoes on the Kates aboard *Akagi* and *Kaga* had to be removed. The planes already on the flight deck were taken to the hanger deck, the torpedoes removed, and bombs put in their place.

At 7:28 A.M. one of the four search planes Nagumo had sent out early that morning reported seeing elements of the U.S. fleet. Nagumo was in a quandary. Half of the Kates still had torpedoes. He canceled the second attack on Midway, and ordered his striking force to prepare for attacks on U.S. fleet units. Torpedoes that had not yet been changed to bombs were to be left on the Kates.

The next American attack against the Japanese carriers came from 16 Midway-based Douglas dive bombers (SBDs) and 11 Vought Vindicator (SB2Us) dive bombers, all operated by the Marines of VMSB-241. Because of their inexperience and/or lack of recent practice, the pilots of both flights had orders to glide-bomb, not dive-bomb, and they approached as two separate flights in long, shallow dives. The gunners assigned to these planes were also green.

The straight, shallow dives left the slow SBDs and SB2Us vulnerable to attack by Zeros. Eight of 16 SBDs and 4 of 11 Vindicators were shot down by Zeros or anti-aircraft fire. Most of those that staggered back to Midway were badly shot up. None of their bombs hit their target, the carrier *Hiryu*.

At almost the same time 15 B-17 Flying Fortress bombers 20,000 feet above the racing Japanese Strike Force dropped their bombs. Water tossed high by the bombs momentarily hid at least two of the Japanese carriers. Not one was hit.

Three Zeros attacked a B-17 and shot out one engine. Another B-17 was attacked, but the Zeros were reluctant to approach too close—B-17s seemed to bristle with guns, and the Zero pilots knew that the big four-engine planes were hard to bring down.

By 8:20 A.M. the B-17s had left, and the Vals, Kates, and Zeros that had

The TBD Douglas Devastator, an all-metal Navy torpedo bomber. The 110-knot planes, mostly without fighter protection, had no chance against the swarms of Zeros at Midway. *National Archives.*

attacked Midway were circling, waiting to land on their carriers.

At about that time the scout plane shadowing the distant U.S. task force radioed that there appeared to be an American aircraft carrier with the formation. Flight decks were cleared, the Japanese carriers turned into the wind, and the planes that had raided Midway were landed. They had to be refueled and re-armed.

Suddenly 15 U.S. torpedo planes appeared on the eastern horizon, flying toward the four speeding Japanese carriers. The planes were from *Hornet*'s Torpedo Squadron 8. Led by Lt. Comdr. John Waldron, they had left the *Hornet* shortly after 8:00 A.M. They were perhaps nine miles from the Japanese carriers when Zeros attacked them.

Gunners in the rear seats of the TBDs did their best, but according to post-war Japanese accounts, there were nearly 50 Zeros. The agile fighters were simply too fast for the 110-knot TBDs. Plane after plane splashed into the sea, but the gallant survivors flew on.

Last to be flying was the TBD of Ens. George Gay. His gunner had been hit, and Gay himself was hit in the left arm. Zero bullets sieved his plane. At about 800 yards from the carrier he released his torpedo manually, for the electric connections had been shot out. He then flew *over* the flight deck of a speeding Japanese carrier. More Zeros attacked, pouring cannon and machine gun fire into his struggling plane. It quit flying and Gay landed in the water. One wing came off, the canopy slammed shut. Frantically he yanked the canopy open as the plane sank. He dived, trying to pull his gunner free, but the plane went down too fast.

Gay inflated his Mae West, grabbed the uninflated life raft and a cushion, and kept the cushion between himself and nearby Japanese ships. He had heard about American pilots being strafed in the water.

He was the sole survivor of the 15 TBDs of Torpedo 8. When night came and the Japanese ships were gone, he inflated his life raft and climbed into it. He was picked up the next day by an American PBY.

Two minutes after the Japanese ships had ceased fire after downing the 15 TBDs of Torpedo 8, 14 more TBDs arrived from the south.

This was Torpedo 6 from the *Enterprise*. Led by Lt. Comdr. Gene Lindsey, they had left the "Big E" at about the same time that Torpedo 8 had left *Hornet*, but had followed a different route to reach the Japanese carriers. Twenty miles away, with the target carriers in sight, Lindsey split his TBDs into two flights of seven each, planning to come in on each side.

The carriers were steaming at 25 knots or more, keeping their sterns to Torpedo 6 to offer a narrower target. It required a 20 minute approach for the 110-knot TBDs to fly close enough to drop their torpedoes.

It was a replay of the slaughter of Torpedo 8, with a repeat of American bravery and gallantry that has seldom been equaled anywhere; Zeros swept down on the sluggish TBDs again and again, and plane after plane splashed into the sea. Yet the survivors pushed on. Anti-aircraft fire added to their misery. Four of Torpedo 6's planes released torpedoes; the other 10 had been shot down.

The Japanese carriers, untouched after seven separate American aerial attacks, were racing northeast, preparing to launch an air attack on the U.S. fleet reported by the scout plane.

Next came Torpedo 3's 12 TBDs from *Yorktown*, skippered by Lt. Comdr. Lance Massey. They had gotten into the air later than the other torpedo squadrons. But Torpedo 3, unlike the others, had a fighter escort. These were six F4F Wildcats of VF-3 under Lt. Comdr. John "Jimmy" Thach. Four of the Wildcats flew from 1,000 to 1,500 feet above the TBDs, which were at about 4,000 feet; the other two were closer.

As a result of the Battle of the Coral Sea, many of Thach's pilots were new to his squadron. Some were *Yorktown* veterans; some had never served on a carrier; others hadn't been on a carrier for months. Some had no experience with and hadn't been briefed on the Thach weave (which at this time Thach called "beam defense"), so painstakingly developed and readied by Thach for just this moment. As they flew toward Nagumo's force, the F4Fs had to do S

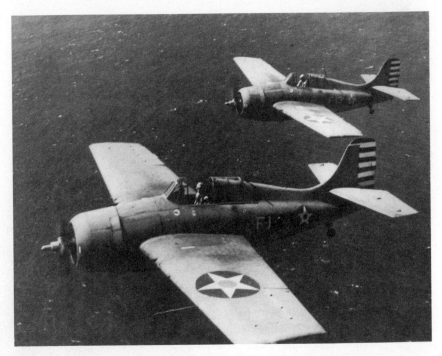

A famous photo of two U.S. Navy F4F Wildcat fighter planes and their pilots, taken 10 April 1942 off Kaneohe, Hawaii. Flying F-1 was Lt. Comdr. "Jimmy" Thach. Flying F-13 was Lieutenant Edward H. "Butch" O'Hare, famed for multiple Japanese kills in the air. Both of these planes were lost with VF-2 in May 1942 in the Battle of the Coral Sea. Thach survived the war; O'Hare didn't. Chicago's airport is named for O'Hare. *National Archives.*

turns to fly slow enough to stay with the torpedo planes.

They were perhaps 10 miles from the escorts screening the enemy carriers when the first Zeros hit them. Thach estimated there were 20 Zeros. Two streams of Zeros attacked; one for the F4Fs, the other for the TBDs. There were so many Zeros they had to take turns to attack. Thach later estimated there was 20 to 30 seconds between individual Zero attacks on his formation.

Then, for tactical reasons, Torpedo 3 split, spreading out in a line, trying to make sure of hits with their torpedoes. This made it impossible for the fighters to protect them.

The closer they got, the more Zeros there seemed to be. There were simply too many Zeros and too few F4Fs for adequate protection of the TBDs. TBDs splashed into the sea one after another—just as they had from Torpedo 8 and Torpedo 6. As the Zeros took their terrible toll, and, as the TBDs neared the escort screen, antiaircraft fire erupted.

Thach and his Wildcat pilots weaved, and the weave began to work. A Zero made a pass at Thach's wingman, turned, and came back, and Thach got a head-on shot at him. He shot another Zero off the tail of the wingman. It was the first known use of the Thach weave in combat.

Five of the TBDs dropped their torpedoes, but only two of the 12 planes of Torpedo 3 survived. The alert Japanese carriers dodged the torpedoes from Torpedo 3 just as they had all the others.

The attacks of Torpedo 6 and Torpedo 3 (especially Torpedo 3 with its escort of Wildcat fighters) had demanded all the attention of the combat air patrol aloft over the Japanese carriers, and all available airborne Zeros had dived to attack.

Most of the planes the Japanese planned to launch against the U.S. fleet were now re-armed and refueled, spotted on the decks of the racing carriers. At 10:20 A.M. Nagumo gave the order to launch when ready, and the four carriers turned into the wind.

It was at this crucial moment that the Dauntless dive bombers (SBDs)

Douglas Dauntless dive bombers at Midway. This famous photo shows a Japanese ship burning from an earlier attack, as two Dauntlesses prepare for another attack. Tail fins of bombs can be seen underneath both planes. *National Archives.*

from *Enterprise* and *Yorktown* struck. They had arrived via separate routes to find the skies high over the Japanese carriers clear of defending Zeros. The combat air patrols of Zeros were far below, shooting down the torpedo bombers.

Lieutenant Commander Thach later described the sight of the dive bombers dropping on the Japanese carriers as "a beautiful silver waterfall."

Akagi took two direct hits; *Kaga* took at least four direct hits; and *Soryu* took three hits. The Japanese carriers had been caught when they were most vulnerable—with fueled and armed planes on deck. Induced explosions of bombs and torpedoes filled the air with flying shrapnel. Gasoline ignited, and great fires spread. Smoke plumed above the three stricken giants.

Hiryu was untouched—for the moment.

Thach lost one of his Wildcats when a Zero shot it down. He personally

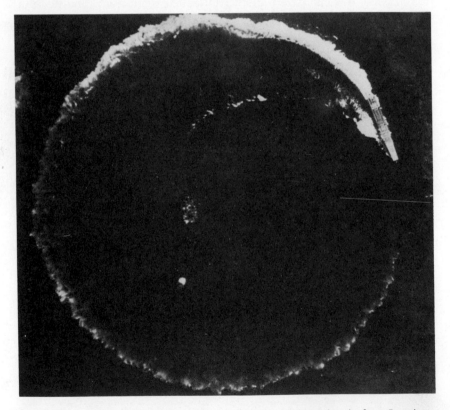

The Japanese aircraft carrier *Kaga* circling in an attempt to escape bombs from American planes at the Battle of Midway, 4 June 1942. After being hit, *Kaga* burned all day, then sank. *National Archives.*

shot down three Zeros, perhaps more. Action was so fast that Thach couldn't keep track. Japanese records indicate that Thach and company "underestimated the number of planes they shot down." The Japanese attributed their losses to "many" F4Fs and claimed downing "many" F4Fs. His pilots were credited with another three shoot-downs. Two other Zeros were damaged by Thach's F4Fs.

Three of Thach's remaining Wildcats flew between the carriers and their defending screen of ships, watching flames and smoke from the carriers reach for the sky. Several surviving torpedo planes appeared, and Thach and his fighters escorted them toward *Yorktown*.

In the 35 minutes from 10:10 A.M. to 10:45 A.M. on that 4 June, 11 of the 41 Zeros the Japanese had flying combat air patrol were shot down, and three were ditched.

At 10:40 A.M. 18 Vals and 6 Zeros left the sole surviving Japanese carrier *Hiryu* to attack American flattops. A dozen F4F Wildcats of *Yorktown*'s combat air patrol met them and shot down 10 of the Vals. At least one other was shot down by anti-aircraft fire. Seven got through, dropping three bombs onto *Yorktown*. Black smoke rose from the carrier, which soon lost way.

Five Vals and one Zero made it back to *Hiryu*, where 10 Kates with torpedoes were ready to take off for another attack against the U.S. carriers. They were to be escorted by six Zeros. This constituted all of the planes now available to the Japanese, who had started with 261 fighters, bombers, and seaplanes among the four carriers. (These carriers also had aboard Zeros being ferried for use at Midway. Total loss of Japanese planes at Midway was 332).

In an hour-and-a-half they found the *Yorktown*, miraculously now underway, fires out or under control. The attacking Japanese believed they had found another U.S. carrier. The Zeros engaged the defending F4F Wildcats, giving the Kates time to deliver their torpedoes; two hit the *Yorktown*. Five Kates and three Zeros returned to *Hiryu*—just half the number that had left.

The Japanese were almost out of planes. *Hiryu* was the sole Nagumo carrier left afloat, and aboard her were only six Zeros, five Vals, and four Kates. The Zeros were sent up for combat air patrol, to protect *Hiryu*.

The sun was near the horizon when the SBDs from *Enterprise* and *Yorktown* arrived. The Yorktowners had fled their disabled carrier to join the Big E. The makeshift flight of determined pilots dived on *Hiryu* from out of the sun at 19,000 feet. The six combat air patrol Zeros attacked savagely, for they were protecting the last Japanese landing place in this part of the Pacific. One Zero actually made two passes at one bomber during its headlong plunge.

The big carrier swung sharply right. The first three bombs missed. But before it was over, sweet revenge! Four bombs hit near the bridge, all from *Yorktown* SBDs. Black smoke rose as fires spread. *Hiryu*, the last of Nagumo's four-carrier attack force was doomed. The Zeros that circled above were also through; their pilots had little choice but to land in the sea near Japanese ships, hoping to get picked up.

Rear Adm. William N. Leonard, USN, ret., was the executive officer of VF-3, Lieutenant Commander Thach's squadron aboard *Yorktown*. He told me, "In all the great air victories of the Pacific war, Midway onward, whenever we neutralized the Jap fighters, we then usually had our way."

Command of the air at Midway was now in American hands. Japanese ships without protective Zeros overhead were within reach of both land (Midway) and carrier planes. The Japanese quickly recognized their danger and their terrible defeat, and fled.

The loss of the four great aircraft carriers was the major turning point in the war in the Pacific. After Midway, the Japanese were mostly on the defensive.

The Battle of Midway has been analyzed for more than four decades. Several things seem clear. The Zero fighter was superior in performance to the F4F-4 fighters. But the ruggedness and heavy firepower of American planes and the tactics, ability, and sheer guts of American pilots more than made up the difference.

"He who controls the air, wins the battles" was an axiom of the Japanese. It was with that belief that they had started the war, believing they had a fighter plane capable of controlling the air anywhere. For a short time at the Battle of Midway, when the combat air patrol Zeros were drawn away from their carriers, the U.S. had clear air. This gave U.S. pilots an opportunity to dive bomb and destroy the first three carriers. By the time they got around to *Hiryu* there weren't enough Zeros to save her.

The Japanese had lost control of the air, and they lost the battle. It was a foreshadowing of things to come.

seven

Heroic Comedy of Errors:
Finding the Japanese Fleet

After retrieving the planes he had launched at Dutch Harbor on 3 June, minus the cruiser float plane that had been shot down, Admiral Kakuta pulled back, refueled his destroyers, and headed west, intending to carry out a reconnaissance and aerial attack on the Aleutian islands of Atka and Adak.

The weather was both his ally and his enemy. A massive search was on for the Japanese fleet, which was hidden by the storm and the eternal Aleutian fogs.

The U.S. Navy twin-engine PBYs, or Catalinas, were intended primarily for reconnaissance, and they were ideal for the job, as they carried fuel for up to 12 hours of flight. The amphibious models (some were true flying boats, without wheels) could use Army and Navy landing strips, and could also land on the water, drop wheels, and waddle onto firm beaches. Seaplane tenders could service PBYs in any sheltered bay.

In April 1942, PBYs assigned to the Aleutians were sent two at a time to the Alameda Naval Air Station, California, where British A.S.V. radar was installed. Crews then went to school to learn how to use the newfangled equipment.

Compared with later radar, it was primitive. Two "hay rakes" (antennae) were installed under the wings, with dipoles all around the hull. The screen was an A-scope presentation; instead of a plan position indicator (PPI) that resembled a chart, it consisted of a vertical range line, and the targets (echoes) appeared in the form of horizontal pips. If the pip waxed and waned, the target was probably an aircraft. A steady pip indicated a ship, land, or other solid object.

The mission of the PBYs was to locate the Japanese fleet and keep radar contact while sending position reports so Army bombers could attack. Navy

Capt. Leslie E. Gehres (now deceased) commanded at Kodiak Island a wing of 24 PBYs that had patrol routes in the Aleutians covering the compass. Even after nearly half a century, those who served under him remember Gehres with feeling. One officer told me, "Gehres was the toughest, most ornery S.O.B. that I ever encountered during my many years in the Navy, but I respected him. He had a war on his hands, and he would sacrifice people and equipment without a second thought if it meant keeping the upper hand on the enemy."

Another officer said, "Gehres was an ogre. We hated his guts."

Lt. (jg) Jean Cusick left the secret Army base at Umnak on the morning of 3 June for regular patrol. About 200 miles from Dutch, his PBY crossed paths with the Zeros of *Junyo*'s combat air patrol.

The swift Zeros attacked before a radio report could be sent, wounding

A PBY at Dutch Harbor, winter 1942. Intended primarily for patrolling, PBYs attacked the Japanese carrier force that raided Dutch Harbor, and later even dropped bombs on elements of the Japanese fleet that seized Kiska. Note radar antennae underneath both wings of this plane, which is being beached by its crew. White objects behind gun blister are canvas sea anchors. *Alaska Aviation Heritage Museum.*

Cusick and wrecking his starboard engine, setting the wing afire. Cusick landed the damaged amphibian, but it was full of bullet holes and soon sank. Three crewmen died in the icy seas after their holed life raft sank. Cusick; his navigator, Lt. (jg) Wylie M. Hunt; and two enlisted men, Carl Creamer and Joe Brown, crowded into a two-man raft. A fifth man clung to a line on the raft for half an hour before he died of exposure and sank. Cusick died of his wound shortly afterward.

The heavy cruiser *Takao* found Hunt, Creamer, and Brown about noon and yanked them aboard. Despite questions from the Japanese—and threats to Hunt that he would be dropped overboard—the three steadfastly refused to divulge where the American fighter base was, although they had taken off from there (Umnak) that morning. The three spent the rest of the war as prisoners in Japan.

When the Japanese first struck Dutch Harbor, Lt. (jg) Lucius Campbell had flown to his dispersion point at Akutan Island, 25 miles from Dutch Harbor. Campbell learned details of the attack over his radio. He took off and was the first to locate and report on the position of Kakuta's ships. Unknown to him, his radioed report of their position and course was garbled.

Zero fighters attacked, spraying his PBY with machine gun bullets, one of which severed the rudder cables. Campbell nosed into a dive, heading for clouds. A waist gunner was hit in the thigh, the starboard gas tank was holed, a fire was started in the tunnel compartment, and a cannon shell carried away the forward starboard wing strut.

Five times Zeros made passes at the crippled PBY before Campbell got into the clouds and lost them. He headed for Akutan. Gas leaked from the starboard fuel tank (port tank was self-sealing, starboard tank was not), and Campbell leaned both engines to their maximum and climbed to give a longer glide when he ran out of fuel.

He got within 40 miles of Akutan and ran out of gas. From 6,000 feet he descended through clouds, rudderless, controlling with ailerons and elevators. He broke into the clear at 300 feet, pulled the nose up, and landed dead stick on the rough sea. Water poured through bullet holes. The crew bailed and drove plugs and stuffed rags into the worst of the holes.

Another PBY spotted Campbell's plane on the water and dropped a note to the nearby U.S. Coast Guard cutter *Nemaha*, which shortly picked up Campbell and crew. The cutter took the PBY in tow, but patches worked loose in the heavy seas, and it sank.

Admiral Russell remembered when Campbell reported to him after the incident. "Skipper, I made a mistake," Campbell said. "When I ran out of fuel and my engines quit, I forgot to cut the ignition, and when I pulled the nose up to land, a slug of gasoline reached one engine, which started." He paused, then said, "But it was the downwind engine, and all it did was to kick the airplane around a little bit more into the wind!"

Campbell was awarded the Distinguished Flying Cross and each member of his crew received the Air Medal.

All that day and night every available PBY searched for the Japanese fleet. Army Air Force B-26s, B-24s, and even a B-17 also searched, almost blindly, navigating by guess-and-by-God (formally called "dead reckoning") through the howling winds, clouds, and fog.

Ens. Jim Hildebrand was swallowed by the storm while searching for the Japanese task force that night. He, his crew, and the PBY were never heard from again.

Admiral Kakuta also had his problems. Thick fog forced him to slow to 10 knots. The farther west he traveled, the worse it got, and the rougher the seas became. He remained inside the storm, using it for cover against attacking planes, and he changed course frequently.

He eventually gave up the plan of attacking Adak and Atka. He had no radar and simply finding them in the thick fog looked impossible. The weather in the direction of Dutch Harbor promised to be better. He decided to finish the job begun the previous day by launching another aerial attack on Dutch.

At mid-morning about 160 miles southwest of Umnak Island, the A scope of Ens. Marshall Freerks's PBY radar showed multiple pips. He had found Kakuta's fleet. He eased below the clouds for a look, then climbed back into them to stay out of sight while he radioed estimated position, course, and speed of the two enemy flattops and their escorts. Freerks continued to trail until relieved by Lt. (jg) Eugene W. Stockstill.

But *Ryujo*'s combat air patrol of Zeros quickly found and shot down Stockstill's PBY. There were no survivors. Bad weather, rough seas, and high winds had prevented launching fighters while Freerks was trailing.

Another PBY pilot, Lt. Charles Perkins, flew from Dutch Harbor armed with a torpedo and two 500-pound bombs. He found Kakuta and made a run on *Junyo*, intending to drop his torpedo. Antiaircraft fire then slammed into the oil tank of his starboard engine. Perkins jettisoned the bombs and torpedo and escaped into the clouds to fly home on one engine. Al Birchman, Perkins's plane captain, reportedly lost all enthusiasm for PBY torpedo runs after that.

Lt. Comdr. James Russell (today Adm. James Russell, USN, ret., of Tacoma), commanding officer of VP-42, a PBY squadron nominally based at Dutch Harbor, was at Cold Bay at the tip of the Alaska peninsula, 180 miles east of Dutch, to instruct Army Air Force pilots in the use of torpedoes. In a tent he shared with Col. William O. Eareckson of Bomber Command, he had a two-man radio crew operating 24 hours a day, receiving scouting reports from the PBYs. He recalled for me those confusing hours of early June 1942.

"If the radio operator got something that looked suspicious, at night he would hit me on the foot and I'd wake up to see what it was. If it looked like we could make an attack, I would call Eareckson," Russell said.

"Finally on that morning of June fourth things seem to work. We had the Japanese fleet located, and we sent Eric on his way. Everybody in his squadron (of six B-26 Marauders—fast twin-engined bombers) missed finding

Kakuta's fleet except for Capt. W. Thornbrough, operations officer of the 73rd Bomber Squadron. He hit 'em right on the nose.

"He made several torpedo runs, as we had taught him, and he told me that the ships turned endwise to him, diminishing the possibility of a hit."

The warhead on a torpedo is armed by a paddle wheel on the side, which functions like the propeller on the nose of a bomb. When the torpedo is released and is running through the water the paddle wheel turns, moving the booster over the detonator. This arms the torpedo. Russell had warned the B-26 pilots that very high air speed might turn the paddle wheel.

Russell continued, "Thornbrough's plane was getting shot up from anti-aircraft fire. He finally dove his B-26 at high speed, hoping to arm his torpedo, then he dropped it as a bomb. He actually flew low over the flight deck of the *Ryujo*."

After the war Russell was assigned to General McArthur's staff in Tokyo. One of his assignments was to interview Japanese participants in the Aleutian campaign. Among others, he talked with Admiral Kakuta's staff air operations officer, Comdr. Masatake Okumiya, who was on the bridge of *Ryujo* when

Comdr. James Russell (*right*) receiving the Distinguished Flying Cross and the Legion of Merit with combat V from Secretary of the Navy Frank Knox in Washington, D.C., late 1942. *National Archives.*

Thornbrough dropped the torpedo. He said that it was an odd-looking bomb, and that it ranged the length of the flight deck and hit the water just under the stern.

"Was there an explosion?" Russell asked.

"Yes, but not a very big one," Okumiya answered. This indicated to Russell that the warhead had not been armed.

Russell continued his recollections, "After he dropped the torpedo, Thornbrough flew back to Cold Bay. He sketched the Japanese formation as he had seen it, and I put it on the radio so all would be informed. He was just like a boy who has been to a candy shop. 'I'm going to load up with 500-pound bombs and go and get those so-and-sos,' he said.

"Although his airplane had bullet holes in it from his first encounter, he ignored them and took off with a load of bombs. This time he apparently did not find the enemy. The last we heard from him he was at 10,000 feet on top of the clouds over Cold Bay."

Russell had a field telephone connected with the tender *Casco* in the harbor. He called the skipper and asked him to use his radio direction finder to coach Thornbrough down.

"It didn't work," Russell continued. "He crashed in the sea on the north side of the Alaska Peninsula. Days later we found some wreckage of his B-26 with the body of his radioman still strapped to his seat."

For a time thereafter, the airstrip at Cold Bay was called Thornbrough Field.

Kakuta's fleet was still untouched. He set course for Dutch Harbor to launch another aerial attack. Part of his assignment was to exert enough pressure so that the U.S. would send ships north to defend Alaska.

Army B-26s based at the secret base at Umnak Island and at Cold Bay blindly sought Kakuta's carriers, ducking in and out of clouds and fog and fighting the turbulence. At times they flew at wave-top height. Poor visibility usually forced them to climb, for they feared flying into the water. But Kakuta's fleet remained concealed by fog, clouds, and rain.

Two radar-equipped B-17 bombers finally found the Japanese. Capt. Jack L. Marks made a bomb run through a break in the fog. His five bombs missed. The other B-17, piloted by Lt. Thomas F. Mansfield, started a bombing run on the cruiser *Takao*, but flak exploded his plane in a roaring sheet of flame.

Shortly, three B-26s found the enemy and dropped torpedoes, two aimed for *Ryujo*, one for *Junyo*. The fish ran hot, and the pilots thought they had made a hit.

They hadn't. Kakuta's fleet went unscathed.

Anxious to attack Dutch Harbor again, Kakuta bent knots on. At mid-afternoon, when about 160 miles from Dutch, he sent 11 Zeros, 11 Val dive bombers, and 9 Kate horizontal bombers off to pound Dutch Harbor.

Flying one of the Zeros was Flight Petty Officer Tadayoshi Koga.

eight

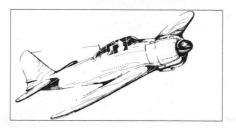

Loss of Koga's Zero

Japanese raiders arrived at Dutch Harbor for the second consecutive day on the afternoon of 4 June 1942. Among the 11 Zeros that attacked Dutch Harbor, along with 20 bombers, between 5:55 P.M. and 6:55 P.M. (Alaska time) that Thursday, was a three-plane Zero section from *Ryujo* led by Chief Petty Officer Endo. His wing men were Petty Officers Tsuguo Shikada and Tadayoshi Koga.

Fifteen or twenty minutes before bombs again fell at Dutch, soldiers at a nearby Army outpost watched as three Zeros shot down a PBY. Dutch Harbor records for 4 June 1942 read: "At 1743 [5:43 P.M.] Fisherman's Point, Army Observation Post reports a Catalina (PBY) shot down in flames near Egg Island. The plane and crew were machine-gunned in the water and all were lost."

The pilot of the downed PBY was Ens. Albert E. Mitchell, USNR. The Army observers had watched as most of the crew of the PBY climbed into a rubber raft as the plane began to sink. They began paddling toward the nearest shore. It was then that the Zero pilots strafed them until all were killed. The three Zeros are believed to have been those of Endo, Shikada, and Koga.

Mitchell's plane, like all available PBYs, was involved in the search for Kakuta's fleet. On the night of 1 June, the engines of the big plane ran rough because of contaminated gasoline, and it was all Mitchell could do to keep airborne.

He struggled to Cold Bay where the right wing tank was cleaned and flushed, but the self-sealing tank in the left wing had too many nooks and crannies for the equipment at Cold Bay to clean.

His commanding officer, Lt. Comdr. James Russell, ordered Mitchell to fly to Kodiak where there were better repair facilities. "Don't come back until you have clean tanks," he ordered.

At Kodiak, Captain Gehres ordered Mitchell to fly immediately back to Cold Bay, Dutch Harbor, and Umnak with dispatches, dirty tank and all.

Mitchell landed safely at Cold Bay. Russell was miffed at his orders being countermanded, but there was nothing he could do about it. "Be sure to call Dutch before you go in," Russell warned. Dutch had been attacked the previous day and could be attacked again.

Ens. Albert Edward "Bud" Mitchell, USN, patrol plane commander of the PBY-5A shot down near Egg Island off Beaver Inlet, Unalaska Island, on 4 June 1942. Zero pilot Koga may have helped shoot down Mitchell's plane. Survivors of his crew were machine-gunned by three Zeros after they escaped in a life raft from their downed plane. It was long believed by some officials that a .50 caliber bullet from Mitchell's plane was responsible for downing Koga's Zero. A 1984 account by one of Koga's wingmates, however, credits ground fire at Dutch Harbor for crippling Koga's plane. *Curvin H. Greene and Adm. James Russell, USN, ret.*

Mitchell *did* radio ahead and was probably told that Dutch was expecting an attack any moment. Instead of flying north over the Bering Sea as he probably would have done with a safe airplane, Mitchell circled over Beaver Inlet where, if he lost his engines, he could land in calm water and drift ashore. Russell thinks his decision was based on uncertainty as to engine performance, as well as considerations for the safety of his crew and plane.

An extract from the war diary of the seaplane tender *Gillis* for 4 June 1942 reads:

At 1948 [7:48 P.M.] received a dispatch from Dutch Harbor that a PBY had been shot down off Beaver Inlet near Egg Island and that the survivors [there were seven on the plane] were afloat in a life raft. Proceeded there at 18 knots and just East of Unalga Island, between that island and Egg Island, a wingtip float with approximately eight feet of wing attached was found. Further searching revealed a life raft unfolded and uninflated with several bullet holes through it, minor debris including a parachute bag and a mattress, and a body that was later

The USS *Gillis*, AVD-12, seaplane tender, warned Dutch Harbor of the 3 June 1942 Japanese carrier plane attack when she picked up the bandits on her radar. *Gillis* also found debris from the PBY shot down by Zeros near Beaver Inlet on 4 June. The *Gillis* was a converted WWI four-stack destroyer. Two boilers (and stacks) were removed to make room for fuel, parts, and supplies for PBY seaplanes. *National Archives.*

identified as W. H. Rawls, Aviation Machinist's Mate First Class, USN. On the body was found the daily flight inspection form showing the airplane to be 42-P-4 and the senior pilot to be Ensign Mitchell—the same airplane and crew that just a few days before we had rescued off Deer Island. Just prior to dark gave up the search for more evidence and returned to Dutch Harbor.

Another American boy was honored by naming a military base after him. The runway at Adak, built later, is still Mitchell Field.

Fate had put Mitchell's plane over Beaver Inlet at the moment that the three Zeros flew overhead.

An account of that day, credited to Petty Officer Shikada, appeared in *Zerosen Moyu* (*Zero Fighter Plane in Flames*) written by Kunio Yanagida and published in Japan in 1984. Minoru Kawamato, a former Japanese military officer who lives in Tokyo, translated for me the three pages attributed to Petty Officer Shikada, who was then employed by a Tokyo bank. Details of Shikada's account do not agree with U.S. records.

According to Shikada's account, the three Zeros of Endo, Shikada, and Koga flew to Dutch Harbor where they strafed two PBYs "anchored in the bay." The big planes didn't burst into flame as the Zero pilots had hoped. Shikada relates that while the three Zeros strafed, Val dive bombers dropped their bombs, and the Kates made level-flight bombing runs.

U.S. records state that bombs hit a beached steamship—the *Northwestern*—and set it afire for the second day in a row; strikes on six oil storage tanks sent more than 750,000 gallons of fuel up in flames; a warehouse and the Unalaska hospital caught other bombs. A bomb went through the roof of the big hanger where Jack Litsey's PBY had been dragged after being shot up during its abortive takeoff the previous day, and where also roosted Lieutenant Perkins's PBY, which had been hit by Japanese anti-aircraft fire the previous day. Four sailors were killed when a bomb struck their antiaircraft mount. Incendiaries ignited a warehouse. Smoke plumed high, and explosions from the oil tanks were heard 40 miles away at Umnak Island.

The defenders had been ready when the raiders arrived, and antiaircraft fire was heavy, though inaccurate. No planes were brought down.

Eighteen Americans were killed, twenty-five wounded.

Physical damage was relatively slight, although heavier than that of the first raid, and Dutch's defenses were still almost intact.

Continuing with Shikada's account, the three Zeros in Endo's group made a second dive at the two anchored PBYs. It was then, Shikada says, that Koga's Zero 4593 was hit "by machine gun bullets fired from the ground." Shikada says his (Shikada's) fuel tank was also hit by this ground fire.

Until Shikada's account was published, U. S. officials had believed that the fatal bullet to Koga's Zero had come from the guns of Mitchell's PBY in the uneven duel near the entrance to Beaver Inlet. It still seems possible that Koga's Zero was hit with fire from Mitchell's PBY, despite Shikada's account. There is no record of two anchored PBYs being strafed at Dutch Harbor on 4 June. In fact, the valuable PBYs had been widely dispersed. Two PBYs anchored in Dutch Harbor would have been sitting ducks to a second Japanese carrier raid, and the VP commanders knew it. Mitchell's PBY was not at Dutch Harbor, but airborne about 20 miles away at the entrance to Beaver Inlet when it was shot down.

Shikada said that Koga's plane spewed oil in a black streak all the way to the tail. His speed dropped and he lost altitude. The spewed oil is consistent with the damage to Koga's plane, for U.S. Navy personnel later found that a .50 caliber bullet had severed the oil line between the oil cooler and the engine. As the engine ran, it pumped oil out of the broken line. It would have eventually drained all the oil, and the engine would have seized.

The oil pressure gauge on Koga's Zero probably gave an abnormally low reading. It would have been consistent with pilot training for Koga to have reduced throttle; with no oil pressure, or low pressure, a lower rpm and cooler running temperature would extend air time before the engine seized. Shikada's report of the plane spewing oil and the speed dropping, with

Dutch Harbor under attack by Japanese carrier planes, 4 June 1942. The permanently beached steamship *Northwestern*, hit by a bomb, is afire and smoking. Building on shore next to the ship is also afire. The *Northwestern*'s engine provided electricity to the naval station, and she was used as a barracks. *Alaska Aviation Heritage Museum.*

Dutch Harbor under attack. Black smoke rises from oil tanks hit by bombs. Other fires rage to the left. *National Archives.*

accompanying altitude reduction, is thus consistent with the known damage.

The three Zeros flew to Akutan Island, 25 miles east of Dutch Harbor, which had been designated for emergency landings. Lying near the island was a Japanese submarine assigned to pick up downed pilots.

At Akutan the three Zeros circled a grassy flat half a mile inland. Shikada thought the ground was firm beneath the grass, but in his second pass he noticed water glistening. He suddenly realized that Koga should make a belly landing. But by then Koga had dropped his landing gear and flaps, and was almost down.

Shikada watched Koga's Zero touch ground, dig its nose in, and flip onto its back. Flight Petty Officer Tadayoshi Koga was about to become a footnote to history.

In 1987 famed WWII Japanese Navy pilot ace Saburo Sakae searched for and found Koga's relatives and learned something of Koga's background. This information was transmitted to me by Lt. Gen. Masatake Okumiya, JASDF, ret.

Tadayoshi Koga was born 10 September 1922 to Shichiro and Fumi Koga in the village of Chitose Mura, Fukuoka Prefecture, Japan, a village about 40 km southeast of Fukuoka City on Kyushu Island. Shichiro was a carpenter whose primary business was making wooden carts and wagons. This business eventually failed, and he went to Manchuria in 1933 and obtained a job at the city of Shenyan as a civilian employee of the Imperial Japanese Army.

Tadayoshi remained in Japan, living at his maternal grandparents' home in the village. He was in the fourth grade of a primary school and wanted to enter the Ukiha Middle School with his cousin Isao. In 1987 Isao recounted something of Tadayoshi's daring as a boy. According to Isao, a tunnel in his village, built about 300 years ago for irrigating rice fields, ran full of water. To boys of the village it was a challenge to dive into and pass through the tunnel, and those who succeeded were recognized as "respectable heroes." Tadayoshi was so brave he accomplished this feat two years earlier than most boys.

Koga entered Ukiha Middle School in April 1936, and when he finished there in 1940 he enlisted in the Tsuchira Naval Flight Training Corps in Ibaraki Prefecture, about 55 km northeast of Tokyo. After completing preflight

Koga's Zero as found by the first American Navy team to reach it. Koga's body was still inside the cockpit when this photo was taken. Note 18-inch diameter plywood auxiliary fuel tank in foreground near plane. *U.S. Navy.*

training, he entered basic flight training, one of a class of 260. Twenty-five of that number, including Koga, were selected as fighter pilots, and in 1942 he was assigned to the Zero Fighter Squadron of the 10,600 ton aircraft carrier *Ryujo*, flagship of the Fourth Carrier Division commanded by Rear Adm.

Fighter pilot Tadayoshi Koga assigned to the carrier *Ryujo*. Koga was buried near where he crash-landed his famous fighter plane. He was 19 years old when he died. *Ushio-Shobo publishers. Courtesy of Lt. Gen. Masatake Okumiya, JASDF, ret.*

Kakuji Kakuta. *Ryujo* was briefly in the Philippines immediately after the war started, and Koga may have had combat experience there.

According to Shikada's account, Endo and Shikada circled, waiting for Koga to get out of the flipped Zero. The somersault may have broken his neck, or he may have received a fatal blow on the head. (When a U.S. Navy party reached his Zero more than a month later, he was still strapped in, with his head hanging in water. He'd have probably survived a wheels-up landing.)

The two pilots were in a quandary. Their duty was to destroy the Zero, now grounded in enemy territory. They had enough ammunition to do so. But they feared Koga might still be alive. Shikada and Koga had been together from early flight training, and Shikada couldn't bring himself to shoot into Koga's plane while Koga was still there. As Shikada hesitated, he noticed he was low on fuel. CPO Endo also seemed to be having difficulty in deciding to fire on the downed Zero. The two pilots signaled each other then set course for *Ryujo*.

The Japanese submarine, notified of Koga's landing, searched Akutan beaches. While it lurked in the area, the seaplane tender *Williamson* detected it and attacked unsuccessfully.

A few days later Ens. Leland L. Davis, flying a PBY, bombed and depth charged a huge Japanese submarine off Tanaga Island, 500 miles to the westward. He thought he had sunk it. Postwar records showed that he damaged it, and that it was the boat that had remained near Akutan Island for several days hoping to pick up Koga. The damaged sub made it safely back to Japan.

After the bombs had been dropped and the strafing was done, eight planes from *Junyo* formed up to the west of Dutch within view of the secret Umnak airstrip at Otter Point. Eight P-40 Warhawks scrambled and attacked. Lt. John Cape shot down a Val, but almost instantly a Zero was on his tail. He climbed and rolled, trying to evade.

He used the wrong maneuvers for escaping a Zero. American pilots still didn't know how to handle the agile Japanese fighter, even though the war was six months old. Developments of this day would change all that. Thanks to Koga's Zero, by November every American fighter pilot in the Pacific would know how best to combat the Zero.

The Zero easily stayed on Cape's tail and shot him down. The runway at Umnak was thereafter called Cape Airfield.

A P-40 flown by Lt. Winfield McIntyre was shot up by a Zero, and its engine quit. McIntyre made a dead stick landing on the beach of Umnak Island and walked away from it.

In the encounter, two Japanese Vals were downed by the P-40s, and two other Vals were so badly damaged that they didn't get back to their carriers.

Aboard *Ryujo*, Adm. Boshiro Hosogaya was in overall command of the campaign to occupy the Aleutians. While awaiting return of the raiding planes, he had received puzzling new orders from Admiral Yamamoto. He was to postpone the occupation, said the orders, and *Ryujo* and its companion ships were to steam south to join Japanese forces near Midway.

Shortly, however, the order was countermanded, and the two Japanese forces in the Aleutians were ordered to proceed with their operations. Then came another change. The Adak occupation was cancelled, and the Adak-Attu occupation force was directed to seize only Attu.

Yamamoto, having suffered a major defeat at Midway, was grasping at straws. Seizing American soil in the Aleutians was a way of salvaging something from an operation that had gone wrong.

Thus ended the second Japanese carrier aircraft attack on Dutch Harbor. They were the only two carrier plane attacks ever made on North America.

Admiral Kakuta withdrew from Dutch Harbor and steamed to an area 400 miles south of Kiska, where, joined by a third light carrier, *Zuiho*, he was ready to support the landings on Kiska and Attu on 7 June.

The two raids did little damage to Dutch Harbor. From the American standpoint the loss of lives was the greatest blow. Kakuta's fleet didn't divert any American power north from Pearl Harbor, and the two Aleutian islands seized by the Japanese had little military value.

The loss to the Japanese of Koga's Zero may have been the most significant part of the Aleutian campaign for both the U.S. and Japan.

The Japanese carrier *Ryujo* was sunk two months later on 24 August 1942 in the eastern Solomon Islands by planes from the aircraft carrier *Saratoga*. *Junyo*, active throughout most of the Pacific campaign, ended the war bomb-damaged and out of action for lack of crew. She was eventually scrapped.

n i n e

Discovery and Retrieval of Koga's Zero

Koga's Zero fighter, a Mitsubishi Type 0 Model 21 (A6M2), serial number 4593, lay unseen in the bog on Akutan Island for more than a month. The airplane was light gray, with rising sun insignia on the wings and both sides of the fuselage. It had one yellow stripe encircling the after part of the fuselage and another at the base of the vertical stabilizer. (See painting on back cover.)

The wrecked plane couldn't be seen from the usual PBY routes or from a ship's deck offshore. Patrol planes seldom flew over Akutan. Fog often covers the island. Only the Japanese knew the plane was there.

Comdr. Robert Larson, USNR, ret., now of Camano Island, Washington, remembers how Koga's Zero was found. In July 1942 he was Ens. Robert Larson, second pilot of a patrolling PBY of VP-41, based at Dutch Harbor.

The other crewmembers were Lt. William Thies (now Capt. William Thies, USN, ret., of Carmel, California), the patrol plane commander; Ens. William Lohse, first pilot; George Raptis, third pilot (enlisted pilot); Harvey, first radioman; Maddox, second radioman; Machinist Mate Knack, plane captain; and Machinist Mate Wall, gunner.

Larson provided me with an account of the events of the flight. The PBY flew a routine patrol south of Dutch, after taking off at dusk 9 July. Navigation was by dead reckoning, with an unknown wind; at dusk it blew strongly from the east, at dawn it was blowing from the west. The night was dark, the sea was rough.

At daylight, with landfall an hour overdue, plane commander Thies feared that the plane had crossed the Aleutians during the night and the PBY was headed north over the Bering Sea; early radar was so unreliable they could have missed seeing the islands on the screen. Larson took an octant shot of the low-lying sun, getting a reading more than four degrees higher than expected. This meant that the west wind had blown the plane more than 240 miles east of its course.

To their relief, the crew soon sighted the Shumagin Islands, which lie south of the Alaska Peninsula and east of Dutch. Weather improved and turbulence decreased so that instead of skirting shorelines, they flew over some of the islands on their return to Dutch.

"While passing over Akutan Island, just to the east of Dutch, one of the gunners, probably Wall, reported seeing an airplane on the ground," Larson

Lt. William N. Thies, 1942. Thies was patrol plane commander of the PBY that discovered Koga's Zero. Thies, holder of the Navy Cross for bombing the Japanese fleet in the Aleutians, has said that, "persuading Paul Foley to let me take a party to the crash site [of the Akutan Zero] was my only noteworthy contribution to the war effort." Joe Rychetnik, ASMP.

recalled. "We passed directly over it and Thies banked the PBY and descended to have a look. The downed plane was upside down, but it didn't look too badly damaged. We marked its position on a map and flew on to Dutch."

Years later, while describing the same incident, Thies remembered his excitement over the find of the downed enemy plane. "I had considerable difficulty convincing our squadron commander Paul Foley, Jr. [now Rear Adm. Paul Foley, Jr., USN, ret., of Manhasset, New York] that we should be released from patrol duty to take a party to Akutan to see if the Zero could be salvaged," he said.

"This was understandable, because we were short of crews and planes

Retired USN Capt. Bill Thies in 1987 at his home in Carmel, California. *Joe Rychetnik, ASMP.*

due both to losses to the Japanese and to the weather. He finally put me in charge of the party to investigate the feasibility of salvage."

Larson's account continues:

"We got aboard YP-151, the *Mary Anne*, a converted fishing boat used for patrol, and went to Akutan Island. We were warned that the Japanese crew might still be around, and to be cautious. We hiked in to the Zero, all armed to the teeth. I carried a Thompson submachine gun.

"We approached cautiously in a slough, standing in about a foot of water, through which grass was growing. From the air the ground looked like a meadow, and the Japanese pilot had landed with his wheels down. That proved to be a mistake. The wheels dug in and flipped the airplane onto its back. He was upside down in the plane, thoroughly strapped in, with his head barely submerged in the water.

"We took pictures and notes, then attempted to tip the plane right side up. It was more than we could handle, and about the best we could do was to prop the tail up so we could get the pilot and his gear out. We also removed

Koga's Zero with the first exploratory party investigating it where it crash-landed on Akutan Island. Lt. William Thies, who was flying the PBY patrol plane from which the Zero was discovered, is in center, hand outstretched, no hat. *U.S. Navy.*

Fog-smothered mountains lie on two sides of the swampy valley where the Akutan Zero crash-landed. The gouge marks (filled with water) in the foreground were made by the wheels of the plane before it flipped. Lt. William Thies (standing behind propeller blade, taking notes) was in command of the first party to reach the plane. *U.S. Navy.*

the 20mm Oerlikon guns from the wings. Our squadron gunner, Chief Petty Officer Duncan, had no trouble field stripping them. We accused him of getting his early training with the Japanese Navy.

"We were rather surprised at the details of the airplane. It was well built, with simple, unique features. Inspection plates could be opened by pushing on a black dot with a finger. A latch would open and one could pull the plate out. The wing tips folded by unlatching them and pushing them up by hand.

"As it lay, we could see but one bullet hole in it, in the vicinity of the oil cooler. The pilot had a parachute and life raft, somewhat discrediting the then common theory that Japanese pilots weren't interested in survival. We could find no sword."

Admiral Russell, who saw the Zero when it arrived at Dutch Harbor, remembers that there were other .50-caliber bullet holes in it, from both top and bottom. "Bullets from above and below is fair evidence of an aerial engagement," he explained.

Was this the result of the engagement with Mitchell's PBY? Russell believes there is much evidence to support this theory.

An Army intelligence team that examined the downed Zero reported, "Bullet holes entered the plane from both upper and lower sides. No holes could be found larger than .50 caliber. The oil return line had been cut by a bullet. The plywood belly tank has a bullet hole from below. There were no bullet wounds apparent in the pilot."

Commander Foley's report to the Chief of Naval Operations, dated 22 July 1942, provides a more detailed description of the condition of the plane:

The plane skidded along for a short distance carrying away the landing struts, damaging flaps and belly tank, and going over on its back, in which position it skidded somewhat farther, damaging the wing tips, vertical stabilizer and trailing edge of the rudder. The plane was resting with the fuselage and engine buried in the knee-deep mud and water.

Koga's decomposed body was removed, a difficult job due to the boggy ground and the two safety belts and rudder stirrups that held him in place. With 15 men assisting, it was possible to raise the tail of the plane only slightly. To release the safety belts, one of the crew crawled into the upside-down cockpit in front of the dead pilot to cut the straps. Koga then fell free.

The body was examined for insignia or anything else of intelligence value. Nothing was in the pockets. Beneath outer clothing, Koga's body was wrapped in strips of cloth. Americans have speculated that the wrappings protected the body, as does a modern pilot's G suit, by helping to counteract changes in pressure that occur during steep turns and pullouts.

Minoru Kawamoto, a resident of Tokyo and a veteran of the Japanese army who has helped with translating Japanese material for this volume, has explained that wrappings such as those found on Koga's body are not uncommon in Japan. They are used even today as a physical and spiritual girding preparatory to physical action.

A transparent plastic folder of several leaves was found secured around Koga's neck. It contained pictures of the latest U.S. Army and Navy planes, simple Japanese voice code, engine power curve, a simple graph for drift determination, and a partially obscured (because it had been in the water and the ink ran) Japanese panel code.

The body was moved away from the airplane and temporarily buried in a shallow grave. There were no tools with which to do the job right.

Lieutenant Thies determined that the airplane was salvageable and returned to Dutch Harbor with that information. He also had some bad news: the wings were integral with the fuselage, which would complicate salvage.

On 12 July a second party, with Lt. Robert C. Kirmse in charge, arrived to salvage the airplane. In January 1988, Kirmse, who now lives in Corpus Christi, Texas, explained to me how 46 years earlier he had reburied Koga's body. He wrapped it in canvas, he said, and buried it on a knoll perhaps 100

Japanese naval pilot's insignia (*top*), and Japanese aircrew badges. These were not from Koga's uniform. Early descriptions of the plane and body do not specifically mention what insignia Koga wore. *Insignia property of Ted Spencer, Alaska Aviation Heritage Museum. Author photo.*

yards from the downed plane. The second in command of the *Mary Anne* gave a little talk over the grave, and then those present said the Lord's Prayer. A small cross made by an enlisted man aboard the *Mary Anne* was thrust into the soft ground at the head of the grave.

Kirmse left Dutch Harbor with heavy salvage equipment and a tractor. With him was Jerry Lund, an experienced rigger, who worked for Siems Drake Construction Company. Lund's knowledge and skills were invaluable, and he was later placed in charge of the third salvage party.

While attempting to unload equipment on the beach of Akutan Island, two of the *Mary Anne*'s anchors carried away, and she was forced to return to Dutch without having landed the tractor.

Kirmse's party worked for two days on plywood islands in knee-deep mud. The engine was partly lifted out of the mud with a tripod. A prefabricated skid made of 6 x 6 timbers was assembled on the spot, but the plane was too heavy to pull onto the skid without a winch. The crew returned to Dutch for more equipment.

On 15 July the third party with Lund in charge left Dutch with a barge, a medium-sized bulldozer fitted with a winch, a second and heavier prefabricated sled, and much gear and lumber.

The bulldozer was landed from the barge through the surf. It bulldozed a trail up a small riverbed the half mile to the plane. With the tripod, the engine was hoisted out of the plane and put on a sled. The plane was then lifted, still upside down, and put on another sled. In lifting the engine and fuselage, the tripods sank three to four feet into the mud.

The Akutan Zero at Dutch Harbor in July 1942. Engine and ailerons removed. Note folded-up wing tips designed so the plane would fit the elevators of Japanese aircraft carriers. Damage to plane from flipping in the tundra bog can be seen at the top of the vertical stabilizer. Yellow stripe around rear of fuselage is concealed by rigging. Yellow stripe at bottom of vertical stabilizer can be faintly seen. *U.S. Navy.*

The two sleds were then dragged to the beach, fording two three-foot-deep streams en route. They were then dragged through the surf and onto the barge. All was accomplished without further damage to the plane.

At Dutch Harbor the Zero was turned right side up with a crane and cleaned. In spite of special guards and precautions it was almost impossible to anticipate every whim of souvenir hunters, and for that reason, cleaning was kept to a minimum.

Chief Aviation Radioman Bryan Franks (later Commander Franks, USN, ret., now deceased) removed all radios from the Zero. He was shocked to find that the radio compass (radio direction finder) was made by Fairchild Aero Camera Company, New York City. The generator taken from the Fairchild radio was an Eclipse, also made in the United States. The plane also had a Japanese-made (Toyo Electric Corporation) crystal-controlled, voice or CW (dot-dash code) radio. It was set on frequency 4145 KC.

The machine gun optical reflector gun sight, the pilot's parachute, most instruments, radio equipment and landing gear aerol struts were reconditioned. The engine and propeller were cleaned and all water removed from the engine cylinders. Several cylinders showed minor rusting, but most were in excellent condition.

Much oil had been lost through the bullet-severed oil scavenger line, but the engine could be turned freely by hand. No self sealing (of fuel tanks), armor protection (for pilot, engine, or plane), destructor devices, IFF (identification, friend or foe, a radar signaling device), or similar equipment was discovered.

Crating of the plane and parts was accomplished as rapidly as possible while awaiting suitable Navy transportation.

The fact that the wings were integral with the fuselage made crating the airplane rather a project. When completed, the dimensions of the crate were such that Foley thought it would be impractical to ship the airplane anywhere by rail after it reached the states (Alaska was still a territory).

The awkward crate holding Zero 4593 left Dutch Harbor aboard the *U.S.S. St. Mihiel*, an Army transport, and arrived at the North Island San Diego, California, Naval Air Station 12 August.

Rebuilding and early flight testing was done in secret. A 12-foot stockade was erected around the plane in the North Island balloon hanger and two marines guarded it 24 hours a day. Repair crews worked 24 hours a day. Repairs, mostly straightening, were needed for the vertical stabilizer, rudder, wing tips, flaps, and canopy. The sheered-off landing struts needed more extensive work. The three-blade Sumitomo propeller was straightened, dressed, and re-used. According to most published accounts, Zero 4593 was ready to fly again by 25 September.

Koga's Zero Flies Again

In 1942 Lt. Comdr. Eddie Sanders was a Navy test pilot at Naval Air Station, Anacostia, near Washington, D.C. In September of that year he received hurry-up orders to get himself to North Island to test-fly Koga's Zero. He arrived a week or 10 days before the plane was ready and watched while the repair crews finished their work.

Today Rear Adm. Eddie Sanders, USN, ret., lives in Coronado, California. A Naval aviator for 30 years, he well remembers those flights of Koga's Zero. "Everything about that Zero was classified 'secret' at first," he told me in May 1988. That explains why his name isn't commonly associated with test flights of that first captured Zero.

"My log shows that I made 24 flights in Zero 4593 from 20 September to 15 October 1942," he said. "These flights covered performance tests such as we do on planes undergoing Navy tests. The very first flight exposed weaknesses of the Zero which our pilots could exploit with proper tactics.

"The Zero had superior maneuverability only at the lower speeds used in dogfighting, with short turning radius and excellent aileron control at very low speeds.

"However, immediately apparent was the fact that the ailerons froze up at speeds above 200 knots, so that rolling maneuvers at those speeds were slow and required much force on the control stick.

"It rolled to the left much easier than to the right. Also, its engine cut out under negative acceleration due to its float-type carburetor.

"We now had an answer for our pilots who were being outmaneuvered. Go into a vertical power dive, using negative acceleration if possible to open the range quickly and gain advantageous speed while the Zero's engine was stopped by the acceleration. At about 200 knots, roll hard right before the Zero pilot could get his sights lined up.

"This recommended tactic was radioed to the fleet after the first flight, and soon the welcome answer came back, 'It works!'

"During the same period (20 September–15 October) I made four flights

Koga's Zero, in 1942 U.S. Navy markings and color, in landing configuration (flaps and wheels down, canopy open) at San Diego Naval Air Station. Pilot was Lt. Cmdr. Eddie Sanders, now Rear Adm. Sanders, USN, ret., of Coronado, California. Short, streamlined radio mast of hollowed-out wood just behind canopy identifies photos of Koga's Zero from those of others of the same model captured later in the war. Others have much longer masts. *National Air and Space Museum.*

in the F4U Corsair, and one flight in the F4F-4 Grumman Wildcat, working with the captured Zero. On these flights Comdr. Fred Trapnell, director of flight testing, Anacostia, flew the Zero. In that period he was the only other pilot to do so.

"While I was in San Diego, I talked to probably 150 pilots who were about to leave for the western Pacific theater, and I gave them the information on Zero weaknesses. Brakes on the Zero were very poor, inviting ground loops. There was no tail wheel lock, only a bungee to keep the wheel straight."

"Was Koga's Zero a good representative of the Model 21 Zero?" I asked Sanders. In other words, was the repaired airplane 100 percent?

"About 98 percent," Sanders replied.

Koga's Zero was added to the Navy inventory and assigned its original Japanese serial number 4593, and so it appears in various U.S. pilots' flight logs and other records. The Japanese colors and emblems were replaced with those of the U.S. Navy.

The captured Akutan Zero in flight. Uncluttered, smooth construction can clearly be seen in this photo of the graceful plane. Holes in front of wings are for 20mm cannon. The two 7.7mm machine guns were mounted above the engine and fired through the propeller arc. Three sizes and shapes of 7.7mm ammunition were in the airplane when it was found, loaded in this sequence: one tracer, one armor-piercing, one incendiary. Note smooth contour of the big radial engine. *National Air and Space Museum.*

    U.S. experts were impressed as they studied this 23-foot-long airplane, for it was a lovely all-metal (except for fabric-covered control surfaces) low-wing monoplane, flush-riveted, with a clean and smooth exterior. Armament was two 7.7mm machine guns that fired 500 rounds each through the propeller, and two 20mm cannons, which fired 60 rounds each, mounted in the wings.

    A flotation bag had been installed in the rear of the fuselage, and there were watertight compartments in the wings outboard of the cannons. The 940 (take-off) h.p. Nakajima Sakae radial engine turned a three-blade constant speed propeller similar to the American Hamilton. The hydraulically powered retractable landing gear placed the wheels far apart, making it stable for takeoff, landing, and taxiing.

    Koga's Zero was built in February 1942, an early production model of the Mitsubishi Type 0 Model 21 (A6M2) fighter plane.

    After Sanders and Trapnell completed their flight tests, the late Capt. Melville "Boogey" Hoffman, USN, (a lieutenant at the time) was assigned to the plane to test it further and to dogfight it against U.S. fighters (see Appendix).

One of the secrets of the Zero's agility was its light weight. With a full military load Koga's Zero weighed 5,555 pounds. In contrast, the Grumman F4F-3, the main U.S. Navy plane flying against the Zero early in the war, weighed about 7,450 pounds with pilot armor and self-sealing fuel tanks. The F6F (Hellcat) then being built to combat the Zero weighed more than 12,000 pounds (the F6F-3 pilot's handbook gives that model's typical combat weight as 12,139 pounds); later models weighed more. A few others: P51B Mustang, 9,800 pounds; the English Spitfire, 6,172 pounds; Messerschmitt 109G-6, 7,500 pounds; and the extreme, the Thunderbolt P-47D, 17,500 pounds.

Critical traits that both Sanders and Hoffman discovered were that at higher speeds the ailerons became stiff and the plane was slow to roll in either direction. Further, the Zero's rate of roll was faster to the left than to the right at any speed, and the engine cut out under negative gravity, as in a pushover into a dive.

Rear Adm. William N. Leonard, USN, ret., flew Koga's Zero in September and October 1944.

Koga's Zero undergoing testing by the U.S. Air Force, 18 February 1943. One of the secrets of the Zero's agility was its light weight. With full military load it weighed only 5,555 pounds. Note short radio antenna—sure identification of Koga's Zero. *U.S. Air Force.*

Admiral Russell recognized the historical value of Leonard's recollections and in 1981 asked Leonard to record his knowledge of that airplane. Leonard did this from memory and by referring to his flight log books. Russell's intention was to file the information in his extensive WWII library.

With Leonard's permission, Russell has allowed parts of Leonard's letter to be quoted here.

Leonard's experience makes him uniquely qualified to describe Koga's Zero and his flights with it. He was a fighter pilot in the Pacific early in the war and saw action in the Battle of the Coral Sea, at Midway (aboard *Yorktown* as executive officer of VF-3, "Jimmy" Thach's squadron), at Guadalcanal, and in the Marshall and Gilbert Islands. He is an ace, with credit for downing six Japanese planes, including two Zeros. In addition to Koga's Model 21 Zero, he flew a Model 52 Zero that had been captured at Guam.

After the war, among many duties, Leonard served for nearly three years as test pilot at naval Air Station Patuxent River. When he retired in 1971, he had qualified to fly more than 50 types of aircraft, mostly single seat fighter or attack types.

Here is Leonard's account of Koga's Zero:

I first saw the captured Zero as a pile of salvage at San Diego shortly after it arrived from Alaska. Soon after, I was sent into the Southwest Pacific and didn't see the plane again until August 1943 when I was assigned as fighter training officer at San Diego.

The Zero had gone to Tactical Air Intelligence Center and was based at Anacostia Naval Air Station, near Washington, D.C. After Sanders, Hoffman, and others tested, compared, and evaluated the airplane, the Army put it through similar paces.

While fighter training officer at San Diego I learned that Koga's Zero was still at Anacostia, airworthy, but unused. I arranged for it to be flown to San Diego. Zero 21 was a mighty sweet machine, even in its superannuated state [by this time the airplane was about 20 months old]. The refined aerodynamic design was not compromised by mass production. Fit and finish of all plates, rivets, the close and accurate fit of fairings, engine cowl, access plates, canopy, and wheel doors was most faithfully executed.

The propeller spinner faired into a cowling that smoothed the contours of the reduction gear housing of the engine. The interior aerodynamics of the engine cowling permitted the adequate cooling of the two-row 14-cylinder engine with a remarkably small intake.

Contrast that with the inlet on the F4F-3 and 4 which originally came with a spinner but had to sacrifice it to cure engine overheat problems. The Sakae engine looked and sounded much like our R-1830. It ran smoothly and cool. Displacement was somewhat less than the Pratt and Whitney 1830, but its 1,130 hp was smoother and adequate. It was not supercharged as extremely as the R-1830-76/86 and at very high altitude (over 30,000 feet) compared very poorly with the Pratt and Whitney.

Top view of Koga's repaired Zero in flight, 18 February 1943. Rear Adm. William Leonard, who flew the airplane in September and October 1944, said, "It flew beautifully. Leaked hydraulic oil. The Japanese radio did its duty but jangled like temple bells in rough air and field landings." *U.S. Air Force.*

But we hardly ever encountered Zeros above 10,000 feet with our F4F-3s and 4s, so we were carrying supercharger hardware as extra baggage. The F4F, which became FM-2, was re-engined with the Wright R-1820 with about the same power as R-1830 but much less supercharger. This was a better machine to fight Zeros with, but we didn't get it in squadrons until 1944, and by that time the Zero was not the problem it had been at the beginning.

By the time I was flying Zero 21 it may have had some of its automatic systems disabled. An example is the automatic altitude compensation of carburetor mixture. The first time I went for altitude the engine began to cut up disgracefully above 5,000 feet. Worried that the engine was giving up, mixture came to mind. On this machine full rich is a rearward position of the mixture control. Manual leaning comes by easing this control forward. On doing this gingerly the engine smoothed up beautifully and the airplane jumped ahead with about 500 more horses—no less.

The propeller was auto hydraulic cum Hamilton—no mysteries. We ran the engine as though it was an R-1830, but did not let the RPM go above 2600. [Prior to 7 December 1941, Sumitomo, a Japanese company, was licensed to build hydromatic propellers under a license from Hamilton Standard. Strangely, the Japanese prop suffered little damage when Koga crash-landed. Photos of the downed plane show two blades of the prop that appear unbent; the third, according to Captain Thies, was likewise in good shape.]

The case of the manifold pressure gauge had been cracked in the crash at Akutan, and it leaked. It was left in the instrument panel, but we used a standard AN type attached to a bracket nearby.

The throttle sat in the quadrant outboard of the mixture control. It was shaped like the handle of a knife—complete with wood side plates for contour. It was about five inches long and on the top had a switch to be operated by the left thumb. This switch was for cutting in or out the 20mm cannon.

The Zero carried many rounds of 7.7mm for the two fuselage guns, and only 80 to 100 [actually, 60 rounds] for each of the 20mm wing guns. Therefore, sight in with 7.7 then cut in the two 20s for telling shots. I dimly remember there was

Koga's Zero, front view, as it appeared when flown by Leonard, photographed in September 1944. The airplane, put into service by the Japanese in February 1942, crashed on Akutan Island on 4 June 1942, and was ready to fly again by 25 September 1942. *Rear Adm. William N. Leonard, USN, ret.*

a trigger lever you could pull up and squeeze on the front edge of the throttle. If you were not in combat, this lever would drop down where inadvertent firing was precluded (we had sad events because the trigger on the stick of U.S. fighters was easily squeezed in excitement).

Cockpit was not so tidy as the F4F but easily as tidy as the early F4U (Corsair) and earlier Vought birds. Instruments were much like ours but metric for pressures, temperatures, altitude. Airspeed was in knots. It had an inner and outer scale as the needle needed to go around about 1½ circles to get to the high end of the scale.

In Zero 52 [a later model] there was an exhaust temperature gauge as well as the usual cylinder head temperature gauge. My guess is that it was a refinement to fine tune the mixture to get the remarkable endurance and range the Zero was famous for.

Gyro horizon had a sky blue upper half like some German WWII instruments I have seen. To the envy of every F4F pilot, the landing gear was hydraulically actuated! [The F4F (Wildcat) landing gear was mechanical—pinion gears and bicycle chain— requiring the pilot to crank some 28 turns from full down to full up.]

Tail wheel fully retracted behind tight doors. Tail hook faired into a recess along the keel. The hook was hinged on the end of its strut, latched in the snatch position to catch the wire then dumped, so the Zero could taxi forward over other wires unimpeded. I understand we toyed with this idea but gave it up because of worries it might misbehave and cause unarrested landings.

Brakes were hydraulic—weak. The wide tread and relatively low landing speed [about 55 mph] favored weak brakes so you might say they were adequate. Rudder bar was center-pivoted with stirrups for each foot. Brakes were actuated by a hand lever; rudder angle determined which wheel received braking action.

The canopy gave a beautiful view of the outside world, noticeably good to the rear in contrast to our VFs [fighters]. The enclosure was made up of many panes of plexi, some contoured. Wind noise was moderate. Some of the enclosure had been destroyed [in the crash on Akutan], and was remade by A and R [Assembly and Repair].

The windscreen section was original, for it bore deep craters from the corrosion that took place during its dip into the marsh of Akutan. These cavities would have a way of coming into focus when air speeds built up. I often wondered why they had not been replaced by A and R. In VF-42 we had some nasty experiences with the original F4F windscreens blowing in on us when flying at more than 300 knots. Grumman corrected it with a beef-up that robbed us of valuable forward vision, but it ended the problem. The Zero had no such heavy structure in the first place, so it was a source of uneasiness.

The Zero 21 had no primer for engine starting. The carburetor had a large capacity acceleration pump you could feel when you moved the throttle. To start, you had the mechanic wind up the inertia starter as you wobbled up fuel pressure and worked the throttle two or three times to spray in the discharge of the accelerator pump. On contact the engine rolled over readily, caught, and picked up to run without complaint.

The carburetor barrel had an oil jacket through which circulated lube oil to combat any tendency to form ice. I'm not sure whether it was always in action or selectable from the cockpit. We never touched it as I remember. Seems a tidy way to handle ice.

In February and March 1945 I had a dandy low-time fresh-caught [at Guam] Zero 52 to fly. It was much like Koga's Model 21, but heavier because of two more 20mm guns. It had a hundred or so more horses, and ejection type exhaust stacks, but flew essentially like the Model 21—very sweet.

Leonard ran into a problem with top brass at San Diego when word leaked that he was planning to fly the captured Zero. Some of the deep

The Akutan Zero, or Koga's Zero (both names are commonly used), 28 September 1944. Most of the shining aluminum in this view is original Japanese structure. U.S. repair was done in anodized sheet aluminum, and is darker gray. A surprisingly small amount of U.S. structural material was involved in repair. After arrival at the Naval Air Station, San Diego, the engine was overhauled, and the bent propeller straightened and hung back on the plane. *Rear Adm. William N. Leonard, USN, ret.*

thinkers decided that flying a Zero (even if it were painted U.S. colors, and sported U.S. Navy insignia) around San Diego would wreck the integrity of the west coast air defense. He had to give prior notice before each flight, and the Zero always had to be in formation with U.S.-built fighters.

In response, Leonard flew only in the immediate vicinity of North Island, deciding that if no one reported a Zero in the air after a few flights, more distant flights would be made.

The upshot? No one ever reported a Zero on the loose in the air above San Diego, and Leonard and company ended by flying the machine when, where, and as they wished, giving Pacific campaign–bound fighter pilots lots of experience in dogfighting with, and flying in, the captured plane.

Other unnamed military pilots who flew Koga's Zero commented on its performance: "Take-off is very rapid. The ship becomes airborne with little effort by the pilot." "The Zero is very stable and has excellent stall characteristics." "The ease with which the Zero responds to stick and rudder pressure is phenomenal." "At speeds where other fighters stall, the Zero is in its element."

American experts had now seen the vaunted Zero, and our pilots had flown it. What did this mean to fighter pilots in the Pacific?

eleven

The Significance of Koga's Zero

"**T**he fact that the Zero from Akutan was recovered, repaired, and flown by our own pilots beginning in late September 1942, the 10th month of a 46-month war with Japan, is of tremendous historical significance," said Adm. James S. Russell, USN, ret. "The menace of the Zero led to some far-reaching innovations in our aerial tactics. That one airplane—Koga's Zero—made possible many improvements in air tactics and in the design of new aircraft and their weapons to be used later in WWII.

"One of my VP-42 crews was apparently lost to the Zeros in Koga's flight, and there is a possibility that a bullet from that plane [Ens. Al Mitchell's] brought Koga down. However, it was the men of VP-41, and particularly their commander, Rear Adm. Paul Foley, Jr. USN, ret., and the patrol plane commander of the discovering PBY, Capt. William N. Thies, USN, ret., who deserve full credit for making the most of this opportunity.

"To me, our recovery of the Akutan Zero so early in the war was a godsend!"

Contrary to some published reports, the Navy F6F Grumman Hellcat and the F4U Corsair were not designed after examination of the Akutan Zero. Both were flying when Koga's Zero arrived in San Diego in August 1942.

Rear Adm. William Leonard, often referred to on these pages, agrees with Russell on the importance of the Akutan Zero. "The best way to understand the enemy and his equipment is to latch onto his hardware and see for yourself how it works," he told me in 1988.

"The captured Zero gave us this insight. After we flew it, instructions went out to our squadrons confirming measures already taken, or prompting new measures, all aimed at exploiting hard facts.

"The Akutan Zero was a treasure. To my knowledge, no other captured machine has ever unlocked so many secrets at a time when the need was so great."

Intelligence summaries that went out to the fleet in November 1942 and to the Army Air Corp in December 1942 confirmed and added to empirical in-the-field experience that military pilots had gained in confrontations with the Zero. The summaries:

■ provided specific instructions to pilots on how to cope with the Zero in combat
■ gave solid information on the Zero. Pilots now knew that the controls of the Zero became stiff when the airplane was flying at higher speeds; they knew that the Zero rolled more slowly to the right than to the left; they knew that the Zero's engine cut out in negative-gravity pushovers.
■ told pilots that the fuselage fuel tank was between the pilot and the engine, and that there was no armor protecting the pilot. Pilots also learned that the three fuel tanks were not self-sealing.

All this was potentially life saving information for pilots who flew combat in the Pacific.

As fighter training officer at San Diego in August-November 1944, Bill Leonard arranged to use Koga's Zero for training pilots who were being readied for combat in the Pacific. They had a chance to fly the airplane, and could dogfight it with their own planes.

"The idea was to give our pilots in their final stages of training a glimpse of the real thing—a preview of coming attractions, so to speak. Those pilots were much better prepared for action than those of us who met the enemy in 1942," Leonard remembered.

Leonard recalled how pilots were instructed to shake a Zero that was on their tail. "The defensive maneuver was to dive, get speed, roll sharply 90 degrees, then pull moderately. The Zero would go zipping by, unable to follow the same path—ergo, our boy got another chance."

P-38 pilots in the Aleutians who met the Rufe, the float-equipped Zero, were told to keep speed at a minimum of 300 mph, and always break hard right and up.

Reason for both instructions? Koga's Zero demonstrated that the Zero responded slowly to ailerons at high speed, and that the Zero rolled more slowly to the right than to the left.

"With the exception of the F4F types, all of our planes had a good speed advantage over the Zero. Our pilots were in an advantageous position as long as they refrained from entering turning contests with the Zero," said Leonard. Even at war's end the Zero could still outturn any of our fighter airplanes, including the latest models.

What was the Japanese view of our possession of the Akutan Zero? Lt. Gen. Masatake Okumiya, JASDF, in his book *Zero*, equated the acquisition of that Zero as "no less serious" than the Japanese defeat at Midway. Midway was a major defeat. So, too, believes Okumiya, was our acquisition of Koga's Zero.

Capt. Bill Thies, USN, ret., pilot of the PBY that found the Akutan Zero, also attaches great importance to that airplane. He told me, "Although my part in its discovery was quite accidental, I have long felt that my persistence in persuading Paul Foley to let me take a party to the crash site was my only noteworthy contribution to the war effort."

Thies is overly modest. He did his share and more during the war, including bombing major elements of the Japanese fleet in Kiska Harbor with a PBY, for which he was awarded the Navy Cross.

"I have been disappointed that the Navy Department never recognized any of the hundred or more personnel who were initially responsible for putting a Japanese fighter into the hands of our own pilots," he said.

A last comment by Thies really says it all: "If our having the Akutan Zero saved even one American pilot's life, it was all worth it."

Epilogue

Koga's Zero came to an ignoble end. About the second week of February 1945 Comdr. Richard G. Crommelin was taxiing Zero 4593 at the San Diego Naval Air station, preparing for a training flight, when a Curtiss Helldiver, an airplane notorious for poor forward visibility when being taxied, overran it. The big Helldiver's propeller chopped Zero 4593 into pieces from tail to cockpit. Crommelin was fortunate to have survived. Perhaps he used up all of his luck in that incident, for he was later killed in action over Hokkaido, Japan.

Thus ended the useful life of Koga's Zero, an airplane accidentally found in an Alaskan bog.

Wreckage of the Akutan Zero was piled in a hangar at the San Diego Naval Air Station. Bill Leonard salvaged from it the manifold pressure gauge, the airspeed indicator, and the folding panel of the port wing-tip. In 1986 he donated these to the Navy Museum at the Washington Navy Yard, Washington, D.C.

A manufacturer's identification plate, once affixed inside the fuselage of that airplane, is now in the the National Air and Space Museum of the Smithsonian Institution in Washington, D.C.

The Zero airplane, of course, is history. Of the 10,580 that were built between 1939 and 1945, reportedly only about 15 complete examples now exist. The National Air and Space Museum of the Smithsonian Institution in Washington, D.C., owns two. One, a Model 52, hangs in the World War II aviation gallery in Washington, D. C. The other, recently restored, is a Model 63 on loan to the San Diego Aerospace Museum.

Other static-display Zeros exist at the Marine Corps Museum at Quantico, Virginia, and at an Atlanta museum. Two, perhaps three, Zeros are on display or are being refurbished in Australia.

A Model 22 Zero, in excellent condition, was captured on Bougainville in August 1945 and is presently owned by the Auckland Institute and Museum in New Zealand.

Four static-display Zeros, none of which is airworthy, are on display in Japan. The one at the National Science Museum in Ueno Park, Tokyo, was found in the sea off Rabaul, New Britain Island, and acquired by Tokyo businessman Minoru Kawamoto. Another, at the Hamamatsu South Air Base of Japan's Air Self-Defense Force, Shizuoka Prefecture, was found on Guam in 1963. A third, in the Arashiyama Museum in Kyoto, was found in 1976 at the bottom of Lake Biwa, Japan's largest lake. The fourth Japanese-owned Zero, in the terminal of the Nagoya International Airport, was brought from Saipan, Northern Mariana Islands, in 1957.

A reclusive Japanese collector has gathered eight Zeros and their Sakae engines from all over the South Pacific. It was reported in 1989 that he was restoring one to airworthiness and expected to have it flying in 1990.

Two airworthy Zeros now exist, both in the United States. One, owned and flown by the Planes of Fame flying museum at Chino, California, has the original Sakae engine and mostly original instruments. It was captured at

Manifold Pressure Instrument from Koga's Zero, salvaged by William N. Leonard shortly after the plane was destroyed at the Naval Air Station, San Diego. In 1986, Leonard donated this instrument to the Navy Museum at the Washington Navy Yard, Washington, D.C. *Rear Adm. William N. Leonard, USN, ret.*

Guam. In the late 1970s that airplane was shipped to Japan where it was flown and exhibited at air shows. It was a popular display.

The second flying Zero, fitted with an American-made engine, is owned by the Confederate Air Force of Harlingen, Texas.

Robert Mikesh, Senior Curator of the Aeronautics Department of the National Air and Space Museum, Smithsonian Institution, told me that the Extra-Super Duralumin (ESD) in the wing spars of surviving Zeros has crystallized so badly in places that it can be scooped away with a screwdriver.

"In every case there is sufficient damage to warrant all these spars unairworthy. The flying Zero in California owned by the Planes of Fame Museum has a new spar that was milled specifically for that aircraft," said Mikesh. Likewise for the Confederate Air Force Zero.

When I started researching the history of Koga's Zero in 1987, both American and Japanese military people I interviewed assumed that Tadayoshi Koga's body still lay in the lonely grave on Akutan Island near the watery

Airspeed instrument from Koga's Zero, salvaged by William N. Leonard. In 1986, Leonard donated this instrument to the Navy Museum at the Washington Navy Yard, Washington, D.C. Note that the needle has to make two circuits in order to register over 180 knots. *Rear Adm. William N. Leonard, USN, ret.*

crash site of his famous Zero. After the war Koga's parents, both now deceased, asked Japanese officials to return his remains to Japan. Their request was in vain.

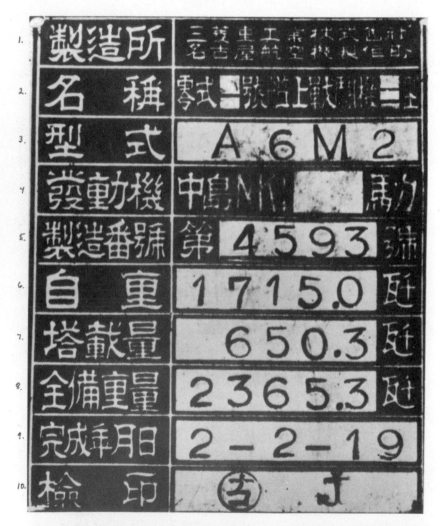

Manufacturer's identification plate that was fastened inside fuselage of Koga' Zero. Translation: 1. Place of Manufacture: Mitsubishi Heavy Industry Co., Nagoya Aircraft Factory. 2. Name: Reishiki Type No. 1 Carrier-borne Fighter Plane, design 2. 3. Model: A6M2. 4. Motor: Nakajima NK1 (   ) horsepower. 5. Manufacture Serial Number: No. 4593. 6. Net Weight: 1715.0 kgs. 7. Load: 650.3 kgs. 8. Weight, fully equipped: 2365.3 kgs. 9. Date completed: February 19, 1942. 10. Inspection mark: 'Na-Ko.' *Robert C. Mikesh.*

Bob Kirmse, who buried Koga, told me in 1988, "I think it would be impossible to find the grave; it has been so long it no doubt is grown over by now." He doubted he could even find the spot.

In 1974 the Japanese Embassy in Washington, D.C., queried the Department of the Navy about Koga's remains. Lee M. Pearson, a Navy historian, wrote Bill Thies asking for details on the burial and if the grave could be located. Thies believed it could not. He reiterated that belief to me when I visited him in 1987.

Two articles I wrote for *Alaska* magazine in 1987 about the Akutan Zero

The Planes of Fame Model 52 Zero at Chino, California, is the only airworthy Zero anywhere that is powered by the original Sakae engine—an advanced model of the engine used in the Akutan Zero (1130 take-off hp compared with 940 for the Akutan Zero). This was one of 12 Zeros captured at Saipan by U.S. Marines in June 1944. Shortly afterward, it was test flown at Wright-Patterson Field. According to Edward T. Maloney, president, Planes of Fame, this plane was made available during WWII to pilot representatives of major U.S. military aviation contractors so they could compare it with their own airplanes. Charles Lindbergh was reputedly among the pilots who flew it. It was due to be scrapped, along with other Zeros on hand at the end of the war, but the Planes of Fame Museum acquired it. This rare plane is flown perhaps five hours a year, and may have had 150 hours of air time since 1978. *Audrey Rearden.*

drew a letter from Minoru Kawamoto, a semi-retired Tokyo businessman and a former Japanese army officer. He was interested in finding Koga's grave and returning his remains to Japan. In June 1988 Kawamoto traveled from Japan to my home in Alaska to arrange for a search for the grave. He would finance the expedition if I could find someone to make the search.

I could find no one at Dutch Harbor or Akutan Village who was willing to do this. Therefore in October 1988, using Kawamoto's money, I flew to Dutch Harbor, chartered a helicopter, and flew to the valley on Akutan Island where Koga crash landed Zero 4593.

Seeing the swift tide, high waves, and violence of Akutan Pass as the helicopter flew over it on the way from Dutch Harbor, I understood why no one at Dutch Harbor was willing to make the trip with a small boat to Akutan Island.

At Akutan Island, I had expected to see a trail in the tundra leading from the beach to the spot where Zero 4593 crashed. Instead I found a swamp, with water from several inches to knee deep, and no tractor trails.

The pilot dropped me and Mike Cunningham, of Homer, Alaska, a helicopter mechanic who had volunteered to help, about three miles inland, in mid-valley. The helicopter was to return in several hours.

Using three Navy photos of the downed plane where it fell in 1942, Cunningham and I were able, by triangulating, to find the precise spot where

The Planes of Fame Model 52 Zero aloft near Mount Fuji while on tour in Japan in 1978. *Edward T. Maloney.*

Author at the original grave of Tadayoshi Koga on Akutan Island, October 1988. Koga, pilot of Zero 4593, crash-landed about 80 yards behind where author stands.
Author photo.

the Zero crashed. Aside from a few tiny ponds where no vegetation grew, we could find nothing to identify the site: no timbers, tractor trails, or debris. That we were in the precise spot there was no doubt. Despite the passage of 46 years, the juxtaposition of willow patches, rocks, snow patches, mountain creeks, and peaks perfectly matched that of the photos from three different directions.

Following Kirmse's directions, I walked to the nearest high ground, perhaps 80 yards toward the beach, and immediately found Koga's grave, a depression in the ground that was from 2 to 3 feet deep, four or five feet wide by 6 or 7 feet long. Loran readings of the helicopter later showed the grave to be half a mile from the beach.

I dug down 8 or 10 inches below the surface in the grave and found a crude unpainted and water-soaked wooden cross. From a photo I sent him of it Kirmse identified the cross as the one he had left at the grave in 1942. I continued to dig. At about 5 feet I came to a layer of hard volcanic material.

There were no human remains in the grave, nor were there any fragments of canvas. Koga's remains had been removed.

I refilled the grave and left the cross where I had found it. It was buried a foot or so under the surface.

Colt Denfield, a U.S. Army Corps of Engineers historian at Anchorage, later informed me that between 1946 and 1949 a graves registration team had remove WWII military men's remains from the Aleutians, probably including those of Koga. To date I have been unable to learn where Koga's remains were taken; they are not in the WWII Japanese military cemetery at Fort Richardson, Anchorage, according to authorities there. Minoru Kawamoto's study of Japanese records indicates they were not returned to Japan. Records of the 1946–49 graves registration team are believed to be in the National Archives.

With nearly half a century gone since Koga died it might seem unimportant to Americans that his remains be found and returned to Japan. That is not the Japanese view, however. It is my understanding that Minoru Kawamoto and other Japanese officials intend to continue the search.

Somehow it seems poetic justice that the airplane we called the Akutan Zero, an enemy fighter plane that probably helped to shoot down Ens. Albert Mitchell's PBY and then machine-gunned survivors in their life raft, revealed to us the important wartime secrets of the Zero fighter plane. The lives of U.S. fighter pilots saved by the knowledge gained from this aircraft were untold in number. The Zero was a fine airplane, but it had its weaknesses. Koga's Zero helped us identify and exploit those weaknesses, thereby hastening the day of America's victory.

appendix

Koga's Zero vs. U.S.
Fighter Planes

From 26 September to 15 October 1942, Koga's Zero was pitted against the best of current American fighters. For the tests, Army Air Force pilots from Eglin Field, Florida, flew examples of the Bell P-39D-1 Airacobra, Curtiss P-40-F Warhawk, Lockheed Lightning P-38F, and the new North American P-51 Mustang to San Diego. Navy pilots flew a Vought F4U-Corsair and a Grumman F4F-4 against the Zero.

On 4 November 1942, the Aviation Intelligence Branch of the Navy Department issued Technical Aviation Intelligence Brief #3, "Performance and Characteristics Trials, Japanese Fighter," describing the plane, giving performance figures and results of the comparison flights with the Navy planes. In December the intelligence service of the U.S. Army Air Forces issued Informational Intelligence Summary No. 85, with the same information for both Air Force and Navy planes.

The following is a summary of the Army Air Force report. Author's comments are in italics.

Performance Figures for Koga's Zero

Altitude	Maximum Speed
Sea level	270 mph
5,000 feet	287 mph
10,000 feet	305 mph
*16,000 feet	326 mph
20,000 feet	321.5 mph
25,000 feet	315 mph
30,000 feet	306 mph

Altitude	Rate of Climb
Sea level	2,750 feet per minute
15,000 feet	2,380 feet per minute
20,000 feet	1,810 feet per minute
30,000 feet	850 feet per minute

*Critical altitude   Service ceiling 38,500 feet (approx.)

A Lockheed Lightning P-38 twin-engined fighter plane. In flight tests, Koga's Zero out-climbed the P-38 from ground level to 10,000 feet. The Zero was superior in slow speed maneuvers. *National Archives.*

Note that the best speed of Koga's Zero was 326 miles an hour at 16,000 feet. This was not particularly fast in 1942. High speed wasn't the reason for the Zero's great combat record early in the war.

Using a standard method of testing, each U.S. aircraft was flown with the Zero to determine comparable climbs, maneuverability, and defensive and offensive tactics. Tests were conducted in 5,000 foot steps from sea level to 25,000 feet.

Take-offs began together, with each plane starting its climb at its best climbing speed. Every effort was made to eliminate the possibility of zooming. (Zooming is a climb resulting from use of residual energy from a dive or from high speed level flight; the lightweight Zero had a particularly good zoom performance.)

Zero vs. P-38F (Lockheed Lightning). Ships [Army Air Force term] took off in formation on signal. The Zero left the ground first and was about 300 feet in the air before the P-38 left the ground.

The Zero reached 5,000 feet about five seconds ahead of the P-38. From an indicated speed of 200 mph the P-38 accelerated quite rapidly away from the Zero in straight and level flight. The Zero was superior to the P-38 in maneuverability at speeds below 300 mph. The P-38 could out-dive and out-turn the Zero at this altitude (5,000 feet) at speeds over 300 mph.

The planes returned to formation and both reduced to their best climbing speeds. Upon signal they started the climb to 10,000 feet. Again the Zero was slightly superior in straight climbs, reaching 10,000 feet about four seconds ahead of the P-38. Comparable accelerations and turns were tried with the same results as at 5,000 feet.

From 10,000 to 15,000 feet the two airplanes were about equal. The Zero was slightly ahead, but not enough to be considered advantageous. Comparable accelerations, speeds, and maneuverability were tried with the same results as at 5,000 feet.

The P-38 started gaining at about 18,200 feet in climbs from 15,000 feet to 20,000 feet. At 20,000 feet the P-38 was superior to the Zero in all maneuvers except slow speed turns. This advantage was maintained by the P-38 at all altitudes above 20,000 feet.

The P-38 proved to be superior to the Zero in a high speed reversal maneuver; it was impossible for the Zero to follow the P-38 in this maneuver at speeds exceeding 300 mph.

The test was continued to 25,000 and 30,000 feet. The P-38 could out-maneuver the Zero due to its superior speed and climb at these altitudes. The Zero was still superior in slow speed turns.

When the P-38 was first used in the Pacific against the Zero, U.S. pilots attempted to dogfight at lower altitudes. That they were unsuccessful could have been predicted from information obtained from the testing of Koga's Zero.

Soon, however, P-38 pilots learned to take advantage of the superior altitude and diving performance of their airplane. They maintained high altitude, then dived to attack the Zero. After firing, they continued to dive until clear, then climbed to high altitude again to repeat the attack if necessary.

Zero vs. P-39D-1 (Airacobra). In the climb from sea level to 5,000 feet, the P-39 left the ground first and arrived at 5,000 feet just as the Zero was passing 4,000 feet. At 5,000 feet, from a cruising speed of 230 mph, the P-39 showed a marked acceleration away from Zero.

In the climb from 5,000 feet to 10,000 feet at their respective best climbing speeds, the P-39 reached 10,000 feet approximately six seconds before the Zero. At 10,000 feet, from a cruising speed of 220 mph, the P-39 still accelerated rapidly away from the Zero.

While climbing from 10,000 feet to 15,000 feet, both airplanes maintained equal rates of climb to 12,500 feet. Above this altitude the Zero walked away from the P-39. At 15,000 feet, from a cruising speed of 210 mph, the P-39 slowly accelerated away from the Zero.

In climbing from 15,000 feet to 20,000 feet the Zero walked away from the P-39. At 20,000 feet at a cruising speed of 200 mph, and from a signal for acceleration, the Zero momentarily accelerated away from the P-39. It took the P-39 30 seconds to catch up and go by the Zero.

The climb from 20,000 feet to 25,000 feet was not completed because the P-39 was running low on gasoline.

In climbing from sea level to 25,000 feet, take-off on signal, the P-39 maintained advantage of climb to 14,800 feet. Above this altitude the P-39 was left behind, reaching 25,000 feet approximately 5 minutes after the Zero.

At 25,000 feet, from a cruising speed of 180 mph, the Zero accelerated away from the P-39 for three ship lengths. It maintained this lead for 1 minute and 30 seconds. The P-39 took 30 more seconds to gain a lead of one ship length.

The rear-engine P-39 Airacobra performed best below 10,000 feet. Few, if any, P-39s saw combat against the Zero. Of the 9,558 Airacobras built, half went to Russia under the Lend-Lease program where the airplane proved most effective in ground-strafing attacks.

Zero vs. P-40F. Tests were not completed with the P-40F because maximum engine operation could not be obtained.

Mechanical problems seemed to plague the U.S. fighters pitted against

The P-39 Airacobra outclimbed Koga's Zero from ground level to 10,000 feet, but the Zero could outmaneuver the P-39 at slower speeds. *National Archives.*

A prototype P-51 Mustang, which became one of the most famous of all Army fighter planes during WWII. In flight tests, Koga's Zero outclimbed the prototype Allison-powered Mustang from ground level to 15,000 feet. The Mustang could dive away from the Zero at any time. *National Archives.*

Koga's Zero. This seems strange; one would assume that mechanically sound examples of our various fighters would have been selected for the tests. Apparently Koga's Zero, battered as it was from its landing on Akutan Island, ran perfectly throughout the tests.

Zero vs. P-51 (Mustang). Climbing from sea level to 5,000 feet, take-off was in formation on signal, but the Zero reached its best climbing speed before the P-51 left the ground. The Zero lifted off approximately six seconds before the P-51 and reached 5,000 feet first with the same lead.

At 5,000 feet, from a cruising speed of 250 mph, the P-51 accelerated sharply away from the Zero.

Climbs from 5,000 feet to 10,000 feet, and from 10,000 feet to 15,000 feet produced the same results, as the Zero walked away from the P-51 in rate of climb. At 10,000 feet, from a cruising speed of 250 mph, the P-51 accelerated sharply away from the Zero. At 15,000 feet, from a cruising speed of 240 mph, the P-51 accelerated away from the Zero, but slightly slower than at 5,000 and 10,000 feet.

The P-51 could dive away from the Zero at any time. The P-51's power plant failed to operate properly above 15,000 feet so the test was not continued above this altitude.

The P-51 was new at the time of the test, and the model pitted against the Zero was probably Allison-powered (the 1942 report doesn't specify which model P-51 was used, only that it was the "new" Mustang). Merlin-powered models, which followed the original Allison-powered ones, had much better performance.

The Mustang saw battle against the zero mostly during the late stages of the war when they were used to escort Marianas-based B29 bombers on missions to Japan. By this time the performance of the Zero—and the Mustang—had been improved considerably over those used in the test flights in 1942.

Zero vs. F4F-4 (Grumman Wildcat). The Zero proved to be superior to the F4F-4 in speed and climb at all altitudes above 1,000 feet as well as in service ceiling and range. Close to sea level, with the F4F-4 in neutral blower, the two planes were equal in level speed. In dive the two planes were equal

P-51 Mustangs on the flightline at the Experimental Aircraft Association fly-in at Oshkosh, Wisconsin, in July 1988. Worldwide, about 100 airworthy Mustangs remained in 1988. *Author photo.*

The Chance Vought Corsair F4U in 1942 was superior to Koga's Zero in level flight and in diving speeds at all altitudes. The Corsair was the first single-engine fighter to outfly the Zero in the Pacific theater of war. The Corsair was far superior to the Zero at high altitudes. These Corsairs, photographed in April 1944, are later models, much improved over the one flown in comparison flights with the Akutan Zero in October 1942. *National Archives.*

except that the Zero's engine cut out in pushovers. The turning circles of the two airplanes do not compare due to the relative wing loadings and resultant low stalling speed of the Zero [i.e. the Zero was superior].

In view of the foregoing, the F4F-4 type in combat with the Zero is basically dependent on mutual support, internal protection, and pull-outs and turns at high speeds where minimum radius is limited by structural or physiological effects of acceleration (assuming that the allowable acceleration on the F4F is greater than that for the Zero). Whenever possible, however, advantage should be taken of the superiority of the F4F in pushovers and rolls at high ' speed, or any combination of the two.

Clearly, "mutual support" refers to Thach weave-like maneuvers. "Internal protection" presumably refers to the rugged pilot-protecting armament and self-sealing tanks of the F4F—the latter installed hurriedly in retrofits after the war began. Except for a few P-40s, Buffalos, and P-36s, the Wildcat was

America's first line of defense against the Zero when the war began, and it was up to these rugged carrier planes to cope with the agile foreigner.

Their success was due in no small part to the quality of American pilots and ruggedness of the Wildcat. Of all pilots in the Pacific facing the Zero in late 1942, those flying Wildcats were most helped by the flight tests of Koga's Zero; that these tests saved lives of Wildcat pilots there can be no doubt.

Zero vs. F4U-1 (Vought Corsair).   The Zero proved to be far inferior to the F4U in level and diving speeds at all altitudes. It was inferior in climb at sea level and above 20,000 feet. Between 5,000 feet and 19,000 feet the situation varied. With slightly more than fighter load, which may be distributed to give equal range and gun power, the Zero was slightly superior in average maximum rate of climb. This superiority became negligible at altitudes where carburetor air temperatures in the F4U were normal; close to the blower shift points, the difference was more marked. The Zero could not stay with the F4U in high speed climbs, however.

The superiority of the F4U at 30,000 feet was very marked and persisted

A beautifully refurbished Goodyear-built F4U-1D seen at the Experimental Aircraft Association fly-in at Oshkosh, Wisconsin, in July 1988. This is a much later model than the one test-flown against Koga's Zero. The Corsair was the first single-engine fighter in the Pacific to outperform the Zero. *Author photo.*

at considerably higher altitudes. In combat with the Zero, the F4U should take full advantage of its speed and its ability to pushover and roll at high speed if surprised. Due to its much higher wing loading, the F4U should avoid any attempt to turn with the Zero unless at high speed, and pilots of the F4U may expect the Zero to outclimb them at moderate altitudes and low airspeeds. In this case, the F4U should continue to climb at high airspeeds and on headings which will open the distance and prevent the Zero from reaching a favorable position for diving attack. After reaching 19,000 to 20,000 feet, the F4U has superior performance in climb and may choose its own position for attack.

The Corsair was the first single-engine fighter in the Pacific to outperform the Zero. Once the Corsair—and the soon-to-follow F6F Hellcat—arrived in numbers in the Pacific, the Zero had little chance unless flown by a pilot of exceptional experience and skill.

Conclusions. The Zero fighter, because of its low wing loading [weight of plane in relationship to size of wing] has superior maneuverability to all our present service aircraft.

It is necessary to maintain a speed of over 300 miles per hour indicated to successfully combat this airplane.

In developing tactics against the Zero, cognizance should be taken of two facts:

1. Slow rate of roll of the Zero at high speeds.
2. Inability of the Zero engine to continue operating under negative acceleration.

The engine performance of the Zero is superior to the present service type engine without turbo superchargers. This superiority is recognizable in the fact that maximum manifold pressure can be maintained from sea level to 16,000 feet.

Recommendations. All pilots entering the theater of action where the Zero can be expected should be instructed in the following:

1. Never attempt to dogfight the Zero.
2. Never maneuver with the Zero at speeds below 300 miles per hour indicated unless directly behind it.
3. Never follow a Zero in a climb at low speeds. Service type ships will stall out at the steep angle at which the Zero has just reached its most maneuverable speed. At this point it is possible for the Zero to complete a loop, putting it in a position for a rear quarter attack.
4. Airplanes to be used against the Zero should be as light as possible—all equipment not absolutely necessary for combat should be removed.

Offensive and Defensive Tactics. The most important features to consider in developing successful tactics against the Zero appear to be its slow rate of roll at high speeds and the failure of its engine to run under negative acceleration.

Flying Characteristics. The large ailerons make the ship [Zero] highly maneuverable at speeds up to 300 miles per hour indicated. Above 300 miles per hour indicated it is virtually impossible to reverse a turn. The rate of roll of the Zero is faster from right to left than from left to right.

An outstanding characteristic of the Zero is its high rate of zoom. This zoom is at a nearly vertical angle and can be continued from 1,500 to 2,000 feet, depending on the starting speed. This should not be considered as indicative of the rate of climb of this airplane.

As shown by the Performance Figures table, the Zero does not possess a particularly high rate of climb.

Of the fighter planes tested against Koga's Zero in the fall of 1942, only the Wildcat faced the Zero at war's beginning; all others were designs under development when the Japanese attacked Pearl Harbor. In a sense, the Zero was already a has-been. Three of the planes tested against it—the P-38, P-51, and the F4U—upon reaching their full potential, demonstrated clear superiority over the Zero in speed, armament, high altitude performance, and ability to absorb battle damage.

The Fleet Air Tactical Unit Bulletin report received by Jimmy Thach prior to the war reported that the new Japanese fighter ". . . climbed at 3,500 feet or more per minute, had high speed, and was incredibly agile."

As Koga's plane demonstrated, the best rate of climb for the Zero was 2,750 feet per minute (at sea level), not really that far from the 3,500 feet reported. Also, "incredibly agile" was accurate, as many a U.S. pilot learned to his sorrow.

At the beginning of the war many U.S. aviation experts believed Japan incapable of building a fighter plane that could compare with those of the U.S. Unfortunately, many of our military pilots believed this, too, and, early in the war, too many of them died from this mistaken belief.

Upon inspecting Koga's beautifully designed and well-built Zero, aviation experts in the U.S. could hardly believe their eyes. First reaction was that the airplane was a copy of a European plane, or that many of the features incorporated in its design came from the U.S. Many U.S. veterans of WWII still believe this.

As we have seen, the Zero was uniquely Japanese; it was a lucky break for U.S. pilots who fought in the skies of the Pacific in the second year of the war that we managed, by flying Koga's plane in the fall of 1942, to unlock the peculiar secrets built into it by the Japanese.

References

Amme, Carl H. *Aleutian Airdales: Stories of Navy Flyers in the North Pacific During WWII.* Pat Wing Four Reunion Committee. Plains, Mont.: Plainsman Publishing, 1987.

Boyington, Col. Gregory "Pappy". *Baa Baa Black Sheep.* Fresno, Calif.: Wilson Press Inc., 1958.

Freeman, Elmer. *Those Navy Guys and Their PBY's: The Aleutian Solution.* Spokane: Kedging Publishing Co., 1984.

Fuchida, Mitsuo, and Masatake Okumiya. *Midway, the Battle that Doomed Japan.* Annapolis: Naval Institute Press, 1955.

Garfield, Brian. *The Thousand-Mile War.* Garden City, N.Y.: Doubleday & Company, 1969.

Jablonski, Edward. *Airwar*, 2 volumes. Garden City, N.Y.: Doubleday & Company, 1971.

Lord, Walter. *Midway! Incredible Victory.* New York: Harper and Row, 1967.

Lundstrom, John B. *The First Team. Pacific Naval Air Combat from Pearl Harbor to Midway.* Annapolis: Naval Institute Press, 1984.

Mason, John T., Jr. *The Pacific War Remembered, an Oral History Collection.* Annapolis: Naval Institute Press, 1986.

Mikesh, Robert C., and Rikyu Watanabe. *Zero Fighter.* London and Sidney: Jane's Publishing Company Limited, 1981.

Okumiya, Masatake, and Jiro Horikoshi with Martin Caidin. *Zero.* New York: Ballantine Books, 1956.

Prange, Gordon W. *At Dawn We Slept: The Untold Story of Pearl Harbor.* New York: McGraw-Hill, 1981.

Sakai, Saburo, with Martin Caidin and Fred Saito. *Samurai!* New York: Ballantine Books, 1957.

Toland, John. *The Rising Sun: The Decline and Fall of the Japanese Empire 1936–1945.* New York: Random House, 1970.

Devotees of literature and movies about WWII fighter plances can purchase a short black and white video (20 minutes) made from a WWII Army Air Force training film that briefly features on-the-wing action photos of Zero 4593—Koga's Zero. In the film, Ronald Reagan plays the part of an American pilot who mistakes a P-40 for a Zero and tries to shoot it down.

Zero 4593 is identifiable in the film by its short radio antenna mast. All other captured Zeros flown in the U.S. had much longer masts.

The video is marketed under the titles "Recognition of the Japanese Zero" and "Kamikaze: Recognization of the Japanese Zero" by various aviation book and video sources.

Index

Note: Italicized numbers refer to photographs.